Real Sweet

Also by Shauna Sever

Pure Vanilla
Marshmallow Madness

WM
WILLIAM MORROW
An Imprint of HarperCollins *Publishers*

Real Sweet

More Than 80 Crave-Worthy Treats Made with Natural Sugars

SHAUNA SEVER

Photographs by Leigh Beisch

HarperCollins books may be purchased for educational, business, or sales promotional use. For information please e-mail the Special Markets Department at SPsales@harpercollins.com.

FIRST EDITION

Designed by Shannon Plunkett
Photographs by Leigh Beisch

Library of Congress Cataloging-in-Publication Data has been applied for.

ISBN 978-0-06-234601-8

15 16 17 18 19   OV/QG   10 9 8 7 6 5 4 3 2 1

For Scott, Caroline, and Andrew,
the sweetest things in my life

Contents

INTRODUCTION
A Word from the Real Sweet Tooth

I HAVE A LEGENDARY SWEET TOOTH. In the way that a college kid might brag of his drinking prowess, I can sugar-imbibe you under the table. Brownies for breakfast, lollipops for lunch. Don't even play; I'll take you down.

But as the years go on, and my body chemistry and palate change, and we add more tiny people to our household who become demonically self-propelled in the presence of all things sugary, I've started rethinking our sweet treats here and there. Not a complete overhaul or elimination—let's not get crazy!—but definitely a shift, leaning into a diet heavily influenced by buzzwords like "balance" and "moderation." Snore, right? Wrong! I'm in it to win it with a real-world approach to desserts and sweet treats these days—tons of flavor, high pleasure factor, just a bit of a rethink in terms of ingredients. And it's been blowing my mind, friends.

Here's the thing: while much of my work to this point has been fueled by a steady stream of granulated white sugar ("Hi, my name is Shauna and I wrote an entire book on homemade marshmallows"), behind the scenes I've spent countless hours playing around with more natural, unrefined, and less refined sugars. What started as an experiment to introduce a few more nutrients into the treats I keep around the house for my husband and our two little munchkins (and, ahem, myself) quickly became a bit of an obsession. Forget nutrients, man! I became positively starry-eyed at the potential of alternative sugars to add layers of crave-worthy flavor and texture to sweets.

* I swapped in dark muscovado sugar and discovered the Bad Boy of natural sugars. Basically dark brown sugar on steroids—rich, smoky, and heady with molasses—it turns out the kind of blondie that bar cookie dreams are made of.

* Turbinado sugar plays the Hero in the natural-sugars pantry; using it instead of white granulated sugar not only gives a flavor boost but also adds a subtle crunch and gorgeous sparkle to streusel toppings, cookies, and quick breads of all sorts.

* Coconut sugar acts as the exotic Femme Fatale in the story of unrefined sugars, accomplishing many of the same results as white sugar in candies while amplifying caramelized flavor with its toasty, almost musky quality (and being a nutrient-rich, low-glycemic sweetener to boot).

* Even white sugar bombs like marshmallows can go au naturel with maple syrup and maple sugar (the Gentle Giants of the natural-sugars kitchen, with their combination of mild sweetness and powerhouse flavor), flipping the script on every campfire s'more experience for the rest of your days.

And that's just the beginning. After years of relying on white sugar's ability to add sweetness to recipes without interfering with other flavors, I made an exciting discovery: the job of flavor-packed natural sugars isn't just to sweeten, it's to *totally interfere*! Equal parts sweetening power and seasoning! Brainstorm!

Soon I was creating an arsenal of recipes—everything from lower-sugar, good-for-you treats that are perfect for lunch boxes and any day of the week, to twists on bake-sale classics that swap out the usual refined suspects for better sugars, to divinely indulgent desserts that outshine the rest of the menu at the fanciest dinner party—but always with a fun, modern (read: not hippie) vibe. These are real sweets with seriously real ingredients, no doubt about it.

Since we'll be spending a lot of time together, let's just get one thing clear from the outset: sugar is sugar. Your body will process every sugary calorie in these recipes in more or less the same way. By no means am I touting the recipes here to be "health food"—this book is decidedly non-diet-y, which is my top requirement of a good sweet treat. You will never convince me that a brownie made with black beans will make life worth living. *But!* I do often notice a difference in how I feel when I have a treat with alternative sugars (the burn tends to feel a bit slower, less crazy-making), and I also like the fact that sometimes I can add a nice little nutrient punch along with the sweetness. But above all, it's about flavor and satisfaction. And we're going to get there with better, higher-quality ingredients, better sugars, and better techniques that work in the home kitchen.

So that's what I'm going to share with you in these pages—a collection of my favorite sweet treats that use the kind of flavorful, natural, less processed sugars and sweeteners that have their place in a balanced life. To me, this is truly baking, and eating, in moderation. Prime your sweet teeth, friends—we're goin' in.

REAL SWEET SUGAR	For every 1 cup (7 ounces/200 grams) white sugar, use . . .	Additional recipe tweaks?
Turbinado sugar	1 cup (7 ounces/200 grams)	None
Light or dark muscovado sugar	1 cup (8 ounces/225 grams)	None, or reduce overall liquid by 1 to 2 tablespoons
Coconut sugar	1 cup (5¼ ounces/150 grams)	None, or increase overall liquid by 1 to 2 tablespoons
Maple sugar	¾ cup (4⅞ ounces/138 grams)	None
Rapadura	1 cup (6 ounces/170 grams)	None
Evaporated cane juice	1 cup (7 ounces/200 grams)	None
Honey	¾ cup for each 1 cup sugar	Reduce overall liquid by ¼ cup
Maple syrup	¾ cup for each 1 cup sugar	Reduce overall liquid by 3 to 4 tablespoons
Brown rice syrup	¾ cup for each 1 cup sugar	Reduce overall liquid by ¼ cup

SWEET SWAPS

I know what some of you might be thinking—*Do I have to buy all these sugars to use this book?*—and the answer is no! Of course, using the ingredients as listed is the best route, but as long as you swap dry sugars for other dry sugars and liquids for liquids, experimenting is encouraged (see "In the Real Sweet Pantry" on page 6 and the sugar profiles peppered throughout the book for tips on the best applications for each). And although you'll have some loss of flavor and color, you can even use conventional supermarket sugars in equal measure for dry natural ones in most cases: white granulated 100 percent cane sugar in place of turbinado sugar, coconut sugar, maple sugar, rapadura, and evaporated cane juice; dark brown 100 percent cane sugar for light or dark muscovado.

In the Real Sweet Pantry

Since entering the world of baking and treat making with natural, unrefined, and less refined sugars, I've tried just about every sticky, sweet ingredient that's out there. In the world of natural sugars, generally the darker the sugar, the less processed and more nutrient dense it is and the bolder flavor it will have. There's a veritable rainbow of natural sugars available (albeit a sort of brown rainbow), both from sugarcane and non-sugarcane sources, and we'll use a wide variety of them in these pages.

Throughout the book, you'll find special profiles of seven different natural sugars, with more detailed information on what makes each one unique and the best ways to use them. But there are a handful of other natural sugars that I love to keep on hand, too. Here are my sweet essentials.

Granulated Sugars Derived from Sugarcane

Using refined white granulated sugar as our baseline (see page 16 for more on the cane sugar production process), let's move through an arsenal of dry cane sugars, going from most to least refined.

> **Organic evaporated cane juice.** Just a few steps less refined, evaporated cane juice is basically white sugar without the final chemical treating, bleaching, and polishing process. So what you get is a slightly coarser, sparkly, blond-hued sugar that has a hint of moisture to it. It's a good starter ingredient for leaning into using less processed sugars in your recipes, as it doesn't mess with the chemistry or texture of your favorite recipes that call for white granulated sugar. It has a really subtle but lovely flavor, almost like a hint of vanilla.

You won't find a ton of recipes in this book that use evaporated cane juice because it falls on the more refined, less flavorful end of the sugar spectrum, but it's a handy, versatile sugar to have available. Most sugars labeled "organic sugar" are evaporated cane juice, and you can sometimes also find it called "natural cane sugar"—just check the label. There's more to be learned about evaporated cane juice and how to use it on page 153.

Organic confectioners' sugar. Again, you won't find a lot of this ingredient in this book either, but it makes for a slightly more natural alternative to the regular powdered sugar you'll find at the supermarket. Organic confectioners' sugar is usually made with evaporated cane juice that has been finely ground to a powder and blended with starch (typically tapioca or potato) to prevent clumping and give loft to the sugar. If you're feeling crafty, you can also make your own confectioners' sugar with other less refined granulated sugars (see page 193).

Turbinado and demerara sugars. A lower-refined, golden-brown, coarse-grained sweetener, turbinado sugar is a favorite of mine and you'll find it in many of the recipes here. In terms of processing, it's a few steps closer to the sugarcane plant than evaporated cane juice. Turbinado sugar can be found under the brand name Sugar in the Raw; the brand's little brown packets on countless café tables and coffee shop counters have helped to popularize this sugar in recent years.

Turbinado and demerara sugars are essentially the same type of sugar with two different names, and they can be used interchangeably. Sometimes these sugars are referred to as "raw sugar" in recipes and cookbooks. In this book, you'll find the term "turbinado" in recipes that call for this type of sugar. Page 105 has more on this Hero of a sweetener.

Evaporated Cane Juice

Piloncillo and Rapadura

Coconut Sugar

Dark Muscovado

Terbinado and
Evaporated Cane Juice

Light and dark muscovado sugars. This dynamic duo is your go-to for powerhouse flavor in your recipes that call for that moist brown sugar that must be packed into its measuring cups. Muscovado is simply sugarcane juice that's boiled down until crystals form, never treated with chemicals, and sticky with molasses. If you like using supermarket-issue dark brown sugar instead of light brown in recipes as I do, then you'll quickly become obsessed with dark muscovado sugar. You can read more of my poetic waxing about this sugar on page 69.

Piloncillo and panela. These hard esoteric-looking cakes of boiled sugarcane juice can be found in ethnic markets, and the name given to them will vary depending on the type of market you're in. In general Latin markets, you'll find it labeled "panela," which is how this type of sugar is widely known across the globe. But shop around and you'll see that Mexican-specific stores will call it piloncillo ("little pylon," as in its cone shape). No matter how it's labeled, it's all unrefined, pure sugarcane juice that's been boiled down, dried, and pressed into disks, blocks, or cones. And to use it, you'll need some muscle and a box grater with large holes. This sugar usually comes in 4½- to 5-ounce hunks and, when grated, will yield about 1 cup of lightly packed sugar.

As tempting as it is, I don't recommend using a food processor for breaking down these cakes of sugar unless you're dying to bust your machine. If you've found yourself with a particularly hard cake of sugar, warm it in the microwave on high power for 20 seconds, and hold it with an oven mitt while you grate it. It definitely takes some effort, but the magnificent brown buttery flavor of this sugar is worth it.

Jaggery and guhr. Two additional names for the same caked sugar, these are Southeast Asia's answer to panela, and they look a whole lot like it. The difference is that these sweet bricks aren't always made of just sugarcane juice; depending on the country in which the jaggery is produced, it also can be made from syrups extracted from a variety of palm trees indigenous to each area, such as date or coconut palm sap. Naturally, each source lends its own unique flavor profile to the finished sugar. But generally speaking, they all offer the same wonderfully earthy, buttery, caramelized flavor and golden color as panela, and must be grated and measured just like panela in order to use them, so feel free to use different solid cake sugars interchangeably in recipes, depending on what's most accessible where you live.

Rapadura and Sucanat. There is great debate over the name of this sweetener; to Brazilians, for whom this sugar is a national treasure, "rapadura" is an age-old, generic term for any unrefined, dried sugarcane juice, whether found in cakes or granulated in bags. In Brazil, you can even find chunks of rapadura sold as candy. But in the late '90s, the Rapunzel sugar company started selling Rapadura (with a capital "R") as a trademarked brand name for dried, unrefined sugarcane juice from the Rapunzel sugar company, which helped bring it to a larger, health-conscious population.

Following an impassioned outcry from Brazilians who took issue with the trademarking of a word so deeply tied to their culture—likening it to trademarking a word like "sandwich"—Rapunzel eventually removed the word from its packaging and now sells rapadura labeled as "Organic Whole Cane Sugar."

Regardless of the producer, I find that when I come across something labeled "rapadura" it's nearly always granulated, with a matte, claylike color. So anytime you see rapadura called for in this book, it's that granulated type to look for. Rich with molasses flavor, rapadura works well in place of white sugar in many recipes, especially ones in which a lot of mixing time can allow the sugar to dissolve. But I also sometimes like to use rapadura in recipes where it's not given the chance to break down, in order to play up its nubbly texture, as on a coating for candied nuts. You can also find Sucanat (a brand name shortened from "*sugarcane natural*"), which is similar to rapadura but usually coarser in texture.

Granulated Sugars from Non-Sugarcane Sources

Coconut sugar. This low-glycemic, nutrient-packed sugar has garnered a lot of buzz in recent years, but has been used as a sweetener in Southeast Asian countries for centuries. It adds a wonderful depth of flavor to all kinds of baked goods and other treats. Coconut sugar companies would like you to believe that this wonder sugar is a perfect 1:1 swap for white granulated sugar in every recipe, but as much as I love this natural sugar and use it in plenty of delicious ways, I don't find that to be the case. You can find more tips for working with coconut sugar on page 43.

Maple sugar. Because it can be spendy and difficult to find (I buy mine online for the best price), I can often be found burying my container of maple sugar deep in the pantry to keep scoundrels from simply dumping it into their morning oatmeal. I hoard this treasure of a sugar, made from evaporated maple sap with a gorgeously bold flavor, for recipes where its flavor can really shine. The lowdown on maple sugar and maple syrup can be found on page 238.

Dates. Dates are a superfood, packed with fiber and nutrients. Some of the nutrients found in dates include potassium, iron, B vitamins, and vitamins A and C, just to name a few. I keep dates in my pantry for a sweet snack, but they're also phenomenal as a truly natural way to sweeten baked goods. When you soak dates in hot water and puree them in a food processor or blender with a touch of the soaking water, you get an intensely sweet paste that not only can replace sugar but also lends fabulous moisture to muffins, quick breads, and cakes (see "On Public Embarrassment and Date Paste" on page 54 for more). You can also find "date sugar" in some natural foods markets—dried dates ground to a fine powder—but I find it to be far from foolproof and not as versatile (it doesn't dissolve), so I don't usually stock it at home.

A WORD ABOUT
LOW-CALORIE SUGAR SUBSTITUTES
AND SUGAR ALCOHOLS

Just to give a quick shout-out to hot topic ingredients like stevia, xylitol, and erythritol: they definitely have a fan club these days, mainly because they offer sweetness with few or no calories and are a more natural alternative to chemical sweeteners. They also cause quite a bit of controversy, in terms of how "natural" they really are. But for me, these sweeteners typically don't find their way into my kitchen simply because they don't taste like much (or can have a weird aftertaste) and don't always bake well, so we won't be playing with them in this book.

Liquid Sweeteners

Honey. You'll see a lot of honey-sweetened recipes in this book and coming out of my kitchen. Nothing beats the ambrosial sweetness of honey when there's a pairing of fruit or nuts involved. But there are other great ways to use honey in baking and sweets, and some other benefits, too, which you can learn more about on page 177.

Maple syrup. Packed with minerals with a more gentle sweetness than honey, maple syrup is a versatile liquid sweetener in the Real Sweet kitchen. I like to play with different "grades" of maple syrup, which vary in flavor intensity, depending on the recipe I'm making. Page 238 has more on this sweet, sticky phenom.

Brown rice syrup. For candies and traditional recipes that call for corn syrup, brown rice syrup is my go-to for a more natural alternative. It has a mellow sweetness that I absolutely love and can be substituted 1:1 for corn syrup, in terms of weight, volume, and level of sweetness. It's also a good direct swap for honey and maple syrup when you simply want to dial down the sweetness in a recipe but don't want to mess up the chemistry of the recipe by changing up the amount of liquid sweetener (a great example of this is the Oat Jacks on page 56, where you can use honey for chewiness, but I prefer a less sweet final product, so I go with brown rice syrup).

   Recently, there's been concern about the levels of arsenic in rice and rice products, so use your best judgment when sourcing brown rice syrup, and as with any sugar, natural or not, consume it in moderation.

Unsulphured molasses and barley malt syrup. Although these dark, strongly flavored sticky syrups are from different sources (molasses being from sugarcane, and barley malt syrup coming from malted barley), I tend to use them both in small amounts and somewhat interchangeably. They both have a similar level of earthy sweetness and a bittersweet quality. Molasses is a bit thinner in consistency and comes in a few different varieties and intensities, but unsulphured is what is most often called for in recipes.

Agave nectar. This liquid sweetener has been entangled in quite the love/hate war in recent years, because some brands of agave nectar have been found to have levels of fructose higher than high-fructose corn syrup (and we all know how much controversy *that* ingredient has caused in recent years). Since the spirit of this book is treating yourself and the people you love with from-scratch treats eaten in moderation, and no recipe here will feature a gallon of agave nectar, there's no need to go into volumes about the pros and cons of agave; as a baker, I will say that I like the mild flavor of agave and the way it behaves in certain recipes, especially in fruit-forward dishes and frozen desserts, and whenever I can, I use raw, organic agave nectar from a trusted source. You can learn a little more about agave nectar on page 199.

Coconut nectar. This bold dark-hued nectar is drawn from the coconut palm and is either bottled as is or dried to make coconut palm sugar. It's intensely flavored, which can make it difficult to work with in recipes, but when you find the right application for it, it's terrific. I especially love making caramel candies with coconut nectar and coconut sugar—it's a caramel unlike any other you've ever had. Because it's low glycemic, it's becoming increasingly popular as a sweetener. It's also especially high in potassium, magnesium, zinc, and iron, and contains vitamins B_1, B_2, B_3, B_6, and C.

Date syrup. Whenever you soak a big batch of dates to make a paste for a recipe, you can also boil down the soaking liquid to a concentrated, intensely sweet syrup that's great for substituting for small amounts of honey or maple syrup, or for sweetening beverages. See page 55 for more.

Honey

Maple Syrup

Agave Nectar

Molasses

Brown Rice
Syrup

NATURAL SUGARS?
UNREFINED, LESS REFINED?
WHAT THE . . . ?

About 80 percent of the world's white sugar comes from sugarcane that's been processed until it's nothing like its original self. (Talk about an identity crisis!) To make it easier to understand what I mean when I talk about "natural," "unrefined," or "less refined" sugars in this book, and since many of the sugars we'll be using in this book are sugarcane-derived, I thought we'd start with a quick tutorial on how the most recognizable sugar—white granulated cane sugar—is made.

That paper sack of white grainy sweet stuff begins life as sugarcane, a bamboo-looking grass that's native to warm, tropical areas of South Asia. These days, sugarcane is grown in more than ninety countries around the world, and Brazil is its top producer. Sugarcane is actually the world's largest crop, with countries as spread out as India, Mexico, Thailand, Australia, Pakistan, the Philippines, and the United States also producing notable amounts of sugarcane. What can we say—we love our sugar and want it bad, no matter where we live!

The harvesting and processing of sugarcane starts off with a bang—literally. To reduce the amount of manual labor required to ready the stalks for processing, the sugarcane fields are set ablaze to burn off any dead leaves and the green tops of the plants. After the fields have been burned, stalks are then gathered, cut, and crushed to extract the sugarcane juice. Over a series of steps, the juice is then purified, evaporated, and boiled to encourage crystallization. After the sugar has begun to crystallize, it's spun in a centrifuge, which results in "raw sugar"; the centrifuging spins off "mother liquor," a substance that is collected and made into molasses. The raw sugar then goes through another process that refines it further, treating it with chemicals to bleach the sugar; remove any impurities, residual flavor, or nutrients; and create finer crystals.

The final result is a pure white neutral sweetener that is quite the magic maker in baked goods, lending everything from sweetness to moisture to brown crispy edges. But with all the processing, white sugar has been stripped of its nutrients, flavor, and unique characteristics that, when given the chance, can really bring something interesting to the party. So stop trying to hide who you really are, sugar! We understand you and love you and accept you in your less processed and perfectly unrefined forms! (I'll stop before we all need therapy and a good cry.)

The funny thing is, for all the bad press that sugar gets these days, raw sugarcane is actually one of the most nutrient-dense plants on the planet, and can be purchased for consuming straight up. It's closely related to wheatgrass and is packed with goodies like vitamins A and C, lots of B vitamins, iron, calcium, magnesium, and antioxidants, just to name a few. (Sugarcane juice shots, anyone?) Obviously the farther along the refining process that a cane sugar gets, the less of that goodness it will retain, which is directly related to the amount of flavor it has. Cane sugars can be pulled out of that process at various points to create vastly different ingredients—the natural, unrefined, or less refined sugars we're talking about here. They're all still sugars with sugary calories and should be consumed in moderation, but they are closer to their original natural source, less messed around with, and full of great flavor, which I love.

So that leads us to the sugars that we'll celebrate in this book—the sugarcane-derived ones captured at various stages of the sugar production process, as well as exciting sweeteners from sources other than sugarcane—from different countries all over the world. They're full of flavor nuances and sometimes have a nice little nutrient punch, too.

Interested in a little Real Sweet tasting experiment? See "Custard in Two Directions" on page 217 for a recipe that really lets you both play with a sampling of sweeteners and school yourself and your friends in the mind-blowing array of flavor notes in natural sugars.

Other Ingredients

These are the additional ingredients I keep in the pantry that work particularly well with natural sugars and will make appearances throughout the book.

Grains and Starches

All-purpose flour. The mothership of flours. Inexpensive, indispensable, and versatile. As with any starch, I like to use it in moderation and when a recipe benefits the most from its lightness and moderate protein content. In this book, whenever possible, I've tried to incorporate some whole wheat flour or nut flour along with the all-purpose flour just to cut down on the refined starches as a complement to the unrefined sugars we'll be playing with. But sometimes certain recipes just don't have the same magic unless all-purpose flour is in the mix, so you'll see some recipes that use it exclusively.

 I develop my recipes using a cup of flour that's on the lighter side in terms of weight. *In this book, 1 cup all-purpose flour equals 4½ ounces, or 128 grams.* If you're measuring by volume instead of weight, measure your flour with the "spooned and leveled" method—use a spoon to gently deposit flour into the measuring cup until it's overflowing and then use the back of a knife to level off the flour.

Whole wheat pastry flour. One of the easiest swaps to make to incorporate a little extra nutrient punch in your baked goods. With its fine texture, it's much kinder on your favorite white flour recipes than heavier, coarser 100 percent whole wheat flour. Some recipes that would naturally have a little more heft and work well with whole wheat's nuttiness, such as muffins, quick breads, and some cookies, come out wonderfully when you swap the entire amount of all-purpose white flour for whole wheat pastry flour. Other recipes do better with a half-and-half mix of both, which is usually a great place to start if you want to try converting some of your old favorites to whole wheat flour and don't want them to come across as too wheat-y tasting. See page 126 for more on my love affair with WWPF.

Just as I do with the all-purpose flour, I develop my recipes using a cup of whole wheat pastry flour that's on the lighter side, in terms of weight. *In this book, 1 cup whole wheat pastry flour equals 4¼ ounces, or 120 grams.* If you're measuring by volume instead of weight, measure your flour using the "spooned and leveled" method mentioned above.

Old-fashioned rolled oats. My love for oats is real and it's deep. You'll see a lot of them in this book because their earthy quality is a slam-dunk with natural sugars. I use them whole, but I also sometimes grind them into a flour to cut back on some wheat flour or to replace it altogether. Toasting oats, either in a dry skillet or in a tiny bit of butter, before adding them to recipes (or even just before making them into a simple bowl of oatmeal) is a revelation.

Cornstarch. A great thing to have in your baker's pantry to MacGyver some homemade cake flour or confectioners' sugar in a pinch (see page 193). It's especially useful to lighten the texture of baked goods made with whole wheat pastry flour. I also love using it to give ice creams and puddings a silky quality without having to add extra fats such as cream or eggs (as in the lovely vegan ice creams in Chapter 6).

Gluten-free all-purpose flour. When I want to avoid gluten, because either I'm baking for a friend or family member who does or I'm just feeling ambitious and experimental, I reach for a premade gluten-free flour blend, preferably one that can be substituted 1:1 for white all-purpose flour and tells you so right on the package, just to make life easier. I keep gluten-free flour blends by King Arthur Flour and Cup 4 Cup (available at Williams-Sonoma stores and online) in my freezer for those occasions when a gluten-free baking moment arises.

Fats

Unsalted butter. Oh, butter, glorious butter! Where would the best baked treats be without it? It's a tenderizer, browning agent, and reliable flavor vehicle. In this book, you'll find plenty of recipes that use it, but in every instance I've been careful to use only as much butter as is really necessary to make the results delicious and worth your time in the kitchen. I go for unsalted butter so that I can control the amount of salt in a recipe, and since salt is a preservative, unsalted butter tends to be fresher, because stores can't keep it on the shelves as long. Although it costs a bit more, I'm a huge fan of organic unsalted butter for baking—there really is a difference when you use the good stuff. One of my favorite ways to highlight the earthy notes of natural sugars is to use browned butter; see page 75 for more information on the nutty, crave-worthy magic of browned butter.

Canola and grapeseed oils. When it comes to a good neutral-tasting, light-colored oil for baking, I usually reach for organic canola or grapeseed oil. As it seems like there's some new terrible information coming out every day about different cooking oils, there's really no one choice that's right for everyone all the time, but for me, these are what I keep in my pantry and recommend in the recipes in this book that benefit from the lovely moisture they lend to baked goods without bringing additional flavors.

Coconut oil. This oil is having a major resurgence after years of getting a bad rap. Though it's high in saturated fat, the word is now that the medium-chain fatty acids in coconut oil are actually good for you, as is the high amount of lauric acid in it, which has antibacterial and anti-inflammatory properties. But I also love the mellow coconutty flavor in certain recipes, and I like to use it in place of canola oil or melted butter when the flavor profile works with other ingredients.

Nonstick cooking spray. Admittedly, this product is not the most natural ingredient you can use in the kitchen. But when it comes to pan greasing, nothing is quicker, cleaner, or more foolproof, and with projects like candymaking, it really is the best slippery thing for the job. I always keep a can on hand for these reasons. However, you can nearly always use butter for greasing cake pans instead of nonstick spray if you prefer, though you may find your baked goods develop a thicker, darker crust when you do this. (You can also fill a small spray bottle with a neutral-flavored oil of your choice.) There are also several brands of nonstick spray made with coconut oil out on the market now, which can be a slightly more natural alternative, as can organic nonstick sprays.

Add-Ins and Other Tasty Bits

Bittersweet chocolate (60% to 70% cacao). This is my favorite chocolate, and one I always have in my kitchen. The higher the cacao percentage, the more intense and less sweet the chocolate will be. In this book, any recipe that calls for chocolate will almost always be bittersweet, with the occasional call for unsweetened chocolate. I love the intensity of a good bittersweet chocolate; it really complements the earthy flavors of natural sugars. There are many brands of chocolate that use evaporated cane juice or raw sugar instead of refined white sugar; the easiest way to spot them is by looking for chocolates labeled "organic." My favorite brands of organic chocolate are Green & Black's and Dagoba, both of which come in a variety of percentages. The vast majority of high-quality dark and bittersweet chocolates will also be dairy-free, which makes them great for the vegan recipes in this book, too, but look closely at the ingredients list just to be sure there are no "possible traces" of dairy.

Unsweetened natural cocoa powder. I call for unsweetened natural cocoa powder in this book, as I find it's the most versatile of cocoas and complementary to natural sugars. Swapping out natural cocoa powder for Dutch-processed cocoa powder in recipes with leaveners might give you different results (natural cocoa powder has more acid than Dutch-processed cocoa, which has been alkalized). For recipes that don't involve leavening—say, hot chocolate or an ice cream base—using a Dutch-processed cocoa powder instead of natural is fine.

Fine sea salt. For me, nothing makes sweet treats more irresistible than a good hit of salt. Fine sea salt is my choice in place of table salt in my recipes. I prefer fine sea salt because it has the same level of saltiness as table salt, but without the sort of chemical, tinny flavor that regular iodized table salt can have. It's an overall cleaner flavor. It's also fine-grained, so it will fall easily through a sifter with your dry ingredients, and it dissolves easily.

Dried fruits. I always look for unsweetened dried fruits, and unsulphured ones often have better flavor and fewer additives, though the color isn't as vibrant.

Nuts. With the exception of roasted, salted peanuts, I like to buy whole raw nuts in bulk so I can easily transform them into whatever I need for a recipe. Use them straight-up raw for snacking or smoothies, toast them dry in the oven, blanch and peel them, salt them or not, add them to candies without the risk of burning them in molten hot sugar. I can also chop them into whatever size I need or grind them fine into a nut flour in the food processor. It takes a little more time to prep raw nuts, but I find a stash of raw to be much more practical and economical. Raw nuts keep for up to a year in the freezer.

Seeds. Unlike nuts, I like to buy seeds toasted or roasted whenever possible, typically unsalted. For my taste, most seeds have a kind of bitter quality when raw, and if I can buy them toasted for about the same price, I will. The exception is golden or brown flaxseeds, which I buy raw and use to make flax "eggs" for vegan recipes (see page 31 for more on this eggless egg phenomenon).

Vanilla beans and pure vanilla extract. After tons of research and developing recipes for my cookbook *Pure Vanilla*, I have a special affinity for high-quality vanilla products. In these recipes where we'll be playing with sugars that have so many different flavor notes—smoky, nutty, bitter, fruity, floral—a touch of vanilla in the background is often the magic ingredient that can help amplify and round them all out. I typically recommend buying the best vanilla extract you can afford, but at the very least, look for one that says "pure vanilla extract" on the label. I like to save pricey whole beans for recipes that allow the pods to be steeped in a hot liquid before scraping out the seeds, such as a pudding, dessert sauce, or ice cream.

Real Sweet Toolbox

These are my favorite kitchen tools that make working with natural sugars a breeze.

Oven thermometer. To make sure that your oven is always the temperature inside that it's telling you it is on the outside. Because ovens lie. A lot.

Kitchen scale. You'll notice the ingredients in this book are listed in volume (cups and spoons) in addition to weight (ounces and grams). Weighing is the preferred method for baking due to accuracy (example: a cup of flour can be measured in many different ways, each resulting in a little more or less flour actually in the cup). I also like weighing for ease, especially for liquid sweeteners. It's much easier to just pour the syrups into the pot or mixing bowl rather than scraping the goo out of a measuring cup.

Parchment paper. Since I most often use it to line sheet pans, I splurge for packs of precut sheets and buy them online. I try to reuse the sheets a few times, flipping them as necessary, for the sake of being green.

Silicone baking mats. These are greener still, as they can be washed and reused. I like these for candymaking especially, because they are heatproof and absolutely nothing sticks to these suckers.

Stand mixer. Although many recipes in this book start out with instructions using a stand mixer, many of them do just fine with a good-quality electric hand mixer (which is also preferred for quick tasks like whipping small amounts of egg whites or cream). Generally, I prefer the power of a stand mixer; with coarse natural sugars, mixing times are often longer in order to break down the sugars. Some recipes really shouldn't be made with anything other than a stand mixer (such as marshmallows, for example). A good stand mixer is an investment that will last decades.

Food processor. Sometimes you can get by using a high-powered blender instead. I put off getting a food processor for my own kitchen for a long time, but I'm telling you, once I finally bought one, I fell in love. I think I might even use it more often than my stand mixer, and for a baker, that's really saying something. With coarse natural sugars and ingredients that need to be finely ground, such as oats or nuts, nothing beats the processor. Make a pie crust in one, and you'll never look back.

Coffee or spice grinder. I am a total coffee snob and grind my own beans every morning, but after a good scrubbing to get out all the medium roast residue, I also use it to grind spices, small amounts of nuts, and flaxseeds for making flax "eggs" (see page 31). Just make sure you clean it well before grinding coffee again (take it from me—you really don't want cumin-flavored anything first thing in the morning).

Scoops of various sizes. I am the scoop queen. I own a few small sizes—a standard-size ice cream scoop (with a capacity of roughly ¼ cup), a 2-tablespoon-size scoop, a 1-tablespoon-size one, and one teeny scoop with a capacity of 1 teaspoon. It's the easiest way to get a proper yield from a recipe, and the fastest way to portion uniformly. I also use them to scoop frosting onto cupcakes before spreading it out, so every cake gets the same amount of icing.

Fine mesh sieve. This utensil is so great for sifting out hard bits from natural sugars and whole grain flour and for straining liquids, such as fruit purees, custards, and infused syrups. It can also be used to sift dry ingredients.

Small saucepan. And I mean small—about 1 to 1½ quarts, max. This is great for browning butter and caramelizing small amounts of sugar. Many of the candy recipes call for cooking small amounts of sugar syrup, and when it's in too large a pot, the sugar can burn quickly, and the syrup won't be deep enough to submerge a candy thermometer in to get a proper temperature reading.

Thin, flexible metal spatula. I'm considering putting my fish spatula in my will. I use this spatula for absolutely everything. Its thin edge allows you to lift even the most delicate cookie off a sheet pan or pancake from a griddle (such as those thin cake layers in the Black-and-White Pancake Cake on page 165).

Small offset spatulas. Nothing spreads batters and creates smooth surfaces quite like these little guys. I have several.

Candy thermometer. Don't freak out over a candy thermometer. They're cheap and so useful in the kitchen. When it comes to making candies, they're essential, and with other recipes with natural sugars, you'll need to cook the sugar to a certain temperature to get it to behave the way you want it to in a recipe.

Ruler. Nerd alert! I keep a heatproof, metal ruler for things like measuring the thickness or dimensions of doughs that need to be rolled out in a specific way. I also use it like a dipstick, checking the progress of boiling liquids and syrups that need to be reduced "by half," "by one-third," and so on. If you lack solid eyeballing skills like me, I highly recommend the ruler.

Flexible heatproof spatulas. For scraping bowls, stirring screaming hot sugar syrups, gently folding delicate batters, and more. I raid the holiday clearance section of kitchen supply stores for these. As long as you don't take issue with using a Halloween spatula in July, it's a great way to get good-quality spatulas inexpensively.

Box grater. The essential tool for breaking down natural sugars that come in cake form, including panela, piloncillo, and jaggery. Do not—I repeat, do *not*—attempt to use a food processor to grate these rock-hard sugars, unless you have a death wish for your machine.

Bench scraper, metal and flexible. Rigid scrapers make working with pie crust and other rolled doughs so simple and keep the dough from sticking to your work surface without your having to add too much flour. The flexible ones do the same thing, with the added bonus of being easily controlled bowl scrapers for really thick batters and other mixtures.

CHAPTER 1

All-Day Snacks and Lunch Box Treats

BALANCE. I'm always trying to figure that one out myself. I do know we all get a little crazy when life gets unbalanced—too much work, not enough play, or too much indulgence and not enough vegetables. You ought to see me after a ten-day holiday confection bender. It is not cute. On the other hand, I also reach *Exorcist*-level crankiness when swinging too far in the other direction. Piles of kale with nary a treat in sight? No can do. I have two small children. You will remove this 3:00 p.m. coffee and cookie from my cold, dead hands.

But herein lies my plight: I want the joy of tucking a little sweet surprise into my kid's lunch box for her to discover, without subjecting her poor teacher to her sugar crash an hour later. I also want my own treats, and I want them to feel like a little indulgence while maintaining my energy, too. So can we walk the line in the sweet treat world? Can we find balanced treats that can propel us toward a more balanced life? I say yes. Now let's go nail that coffee break.

Breakfast Cookies

MAKES NINE 3-INCH COOKIES

Before I had children, I swore up and down that I'd never be one of those parents kowtowing to the little picky eaters' preferences at mealtimes. And then I had actual children. I'm no parenting expert, but my personal studies have shown that anytime you can legitimately make a meal out of a cookie and milk, you're golden. As it happens, grown-ups won't turn these down, either. And, bonus! When made with flax "eggs" and gluten-free oats, these wholesome gems are vegan and gluten-free.

1 tablespoon (⅜ ounce/11 grams) golden flaxseeds, or 1 whole large egg

3 tablespoons (1½ ounces/43 grams) hot water

1½ cups (5¼ ounces/150 grams) old-fashioned rolled oats

¾ cup (4½ ounces/128 grams) cooked quinoa

¼ cup (¾ ounce/20 grams) unsweetened shredded coconut or finely chopped nuts

½ teaspoon ground cinnamon

½ teaspoon baking powder

½ teaspoon fine sea salt

¼ teaspoon baking soda

⅓ cup (3 ounces/85 grams) Date Paste* (see page 53)

⅓ cup (2⅝ ounces/75 grams) coconut or canola oil

¼ cup (3 ounces/85 grams) pure maple syrup

½ teaspoon pure vanilla extract

½ cup (2⅞ ounces/80 grams) chopped dried fruit**

1. Position a rack in the center of the oven and preheat the oven to 350°F. Line a baking sheet with parchment paper or a silicone baking mat.

2. If using a flax "egg," in a clean coffee or spice grinder, process the flaxseeds to a fine powder. In a small bowl, whisk together the flax powder and water. Set aside to thicken for 10 minutes, whisking occasionally; it should be thick and viscous and the consistency of a beaten egg. (See page 31 for more details on making flax "eggs.")

3. In the bowl of a food processor fitted with the steel blade, process ¾ cup (2⅝ ounces/75 grams) of the oats to a flour (a few tweedy bits here and there, without any whole oats in the mix, are fine). Transfer the oat flour to a large bowl. To the bowl, add the remaining oats, the quinoa, coconut, cinnamon, baking powder, salt, and baking soda. Whisk to blend.

* If you want to forgo making the date paste, swap in ⅓ cup well-mashed very ripe banana (about 1 medium banana).

** I love a combination of golden raisins, chopped dried apricots, and dried cranberries (orange-flavored dried cranberries are especially good here, if you can get them).

4. In the food processor, combine the date paste, oil, maple syrup, and vanilla extract. Add the flax "egg" (or whole egg, if using) to the processor and blend until slightly aerated, 1 full minute.

5. Scrape the wet ingredients into the bowl with the dry ingredients and stir until the dough is evenly moistened. Fold in the dried fruit. Let the dough rest for 10 minutes.

6. Using a standard ice cream scoop, drop 9 quarter cupfuls of the dough onto the prepared baking sheet, spacing them evenly. Use your fingertips to flatten each cookie to a ½-inch thickness—the cookies will not spread much during baking. Bake until golden, about 30 minutes. You'll know they're done when their fragrance fills the kitchen, and the cookies are set enough that you can lift one off the sheet to make sure the bottom is a deep golden color, though the centers will still be soft.

7. Cool the cookies on the baking sheet for 5 minutes before transferring to a wire rack to cool completely. Store in an airtight container for up to 3 days.

TIP: *If you're not a quinoa fan, or are too short on time to cook a batch, just eliminate the quinoa and up the amount of oats to 2 cups (7 ounces/200 grams), still only grinding ¾ cup (2⅝ ounces/75 grams) of the oats to a flour.*

The Fabulous Flax Egg

I can hear my relatives in Illinois now: "What on earth is a flax egg?" Well. Let me tell you about a little something that completely changed the way I bake for my vegan and egg-free friends and also happens to work really well with many recipes using natural sugars.

In my pre–flax egg life, I'd use a packaged egg replacer when trying to convert recipes to be eggless. But it's expensive and has additives. I keep whole flaxseeds in my freezer for a nutrition boost in smoothies and baked treats, and one day I learned that you can make them behave a whole lot like eggs in many recipes, without actually using . . . eggs. So how do we make a flax egg, exactly? Simple.

1 tablespoon finely ground flaxseeds **+** 3 tablespoons (1½ ounces/43 grams) hot water **+** 10-minute soak **= 1 FLAX EGG**

To substitute 1 whole large egg, place 1 tablespoon flaxseeds in a clean coffee grinder or spice grinder. Process to a fine powder. Dump the powder into a small bowl and whisk in 3 tablespoons of hot water. Let the mixture rest for 10 minutes. It will thicken to the consistency of a well-beaten egg—the result of the flaxseeds' starches coming in contact with liquid. These starches help emulsify or "bind" a batter, provide mild structure, and can even provide a tiny bit of air or "lift" to baked goods.

A few things to keep in mind when working with flax eggs:

1. You can buy ground flaxseeds, but the results are much better when you grind them fresh.

2. The best recipes for using flax eggs are quick breads and muffins, cakes that don't need to be super fluffy, and cookies.

3. Some recipes rely solely on the protein in eggs to trap air during mixing, for both structure and leavening—as in an angel food cake or a meringue. Flax eggs won't work in these types of recipes.

4. Recipes that call for more than 3 eggs get a little iffy for swapping in flax eggs—that's a sign that the structure of the baked good is relying on egg protein.

5. I like golden flax for its mild flavor and lighter color, but the more flax eggs you use in a recipe, the more you risk tasting a bitter "flaxiness." Also note that even when you use golden flaxseeds, you will see flecks of seed in the finished baked good if the rest of the item is lightly colored; so there are aesthetic considerations as well.

Apricot, Cranberry, and Almond Whipped Cream Scones

MAKES 8 LARGE OR 12 SMALLER SCONES

For the longest time, I was never really a scone person. To me, they were all too often leaden and dry, and neither sweet nor savory enough to be a baked good winner. But as it turned out, I'd just been having the *wrong* scones. Done right—made with a light touch, tasty add-ins, and just the right amount of honeyed sweetness and turbinado for sparkle and crunch—it's a totally different, delicious story. Using a cloud of whipped cream, rather than just pouring in the liquid version, gives them additional lightness and a melting quality.

SCONE DOUGH

½ cup (2⅞ ounces/80 grams) dried apricots, diced

¼ cup (1⅜ ounces/40 grams) dried cranberries

2 tablespoons (1 ounce/28 grams) water

½ teaspoon pure vanilla extract

¼ teaspoon pure almond extract

1 cup (4¼ ounces/120 grams) whole wheat pastry flour, spooned and leveled

1 cup (4½ ounces/128 grams) unbleached all-purpose flour, spooned and leveled, plus more for dusting

1 tablespoon baking powder

2 teaspoons finely grated orange zest*****

½ teaspoon fine sea salt

6 tablespoons (3 ounces/85 grams) very cold unsalted butter, cut into ¼-inch pieces

1. Position a rack in the center of the oven and preheat the oven to 425°F. Line a baking sheet with parchment paper. Have ready an 8-inch round cake pan.

2. In a small, heatproof bowl, combine the apricots, cranberries, water, vanilla extract, and almond extract. Heat in the microwave on high power until steaming, about 45 seconds. Cover the bowl with plastic wrap or a clean tea towel and set aside.

3. In a large bowl, whisk together the pastry and all-purpose flours, baking powder, orange zest, and salt. Add the butter. Using your fingertips, rub the butter into the dry ingredients until the mixture resembles a coarse meal without any obvious little chunks of butter in the mix.

* Whenever I use citrus zest in a recipe, I reach for unwaxed, organic fruit.

⅓ cup (1¼ ounces/34 grams) sliced almonds

1 cup (8½ ounces/240 grams) chilled heavy cream

2 tablespoons (1½ ounces/42 grams) honey

FINISHING THE SCONES

1 large egg

1 tablespoon water

Turbinado sugar, for sprinkling

TIP: *This dough is a sticky one, but it leads to moist, fluffy baked scones. To keep the stick factor down, not enough can be said about keeping the dough as cool as possible while it comes together and not overworking it—a bench scraper is really helpful for keeping the dough moving on the board without having to squish it with warm hands or add too much flour.*

4. Uncover the bowl of dried fruit bits. The fruit should be nicely plumped without much liquid in the bowl (drain off any excess). Lightly pat the fruit dry with paper toweling. Add the fruit bits and the almonds to the dry ingredients and toss with your hands to combine.

5. In a medium bowl, combine the heavy cream and honey. Using a handheld mixer, beat the cream to soft peaks.

6. Using a large, flexible spatula, gently fold the honeyed whipped cream into the flour mixture; it will look quite dry at first, but after several folds the dough will begin to come together. When no large puffs of cream remain visible, stop folding—don't overmix.

7. Lightly flour a work surface, and turn out the dough onto it—the dough will be soft and sticky. Gently knead the dough 5 or 6 times just to smooth it out. Pat the dough into a disk about 6 inches across. Dust a little more flour onto the top of the disk and invert it, flour side down, into the cake pan. Press the dough evenly into the pan to shape it into a neat circle. Dust the top lightly with flour. Invert the molded dough back out onto the work surface. Using a bench scraper or large knife, cut the circle into 8 large wedges. Place the scones, evenly spaced, onto the prepared baking sheet.

8. To finish the scones, in a small bowl whisk together the egg with the water until smooth. Using a pastry brush, lightly brush the scones with the egg wash, followed by a generous sprinkling of sugar.

9. Bake until the scones are golden all over, about 15 minutes. Transfer to a wire rack to cool. Serve slightly warm or at room temperature.

Baked Apple-Cinnamon Doughnuts

MAKES 1 DOZEN DOUGHNUTS

Let's be real—baked doughnuts are really just cake in the shape of a doughnut. But if you can make them with whole wheat flour, use a flavorful natural sugar, and get some fruit into them, you're a little closer to legitimately having dessert for breakfast. Hooray!

2 cups (8½ ounces/240 grams) whole wheat pastry flour, spooned and leveled

2 teaspoons baking powder

¾ teaspoon fine sea salt

¾ teaspoon ground cinnamon

½ teaspoon freshly grated nutmeg

2 large eggs

⅔ cup (3½ ounces/100 grams) coconut sugar

½ cup (4 ounces/113 grams) grapeseed or canola oil

⅔ cup (5⅝ ounces/160 grams) whole milk

½ teaspoon pure vanilla extract

1 medium Granny Smith apple, peeled, cored, and cut into ¼-inch dice

1. Position a rack in the center of the oven and preheat the oven to 425°F. Spray the wells of a 6-cup doughnut pan with nonstick cooking spray.

2. In a medium bowl, whisk together the flour, baking powder, salt, cinnamon, and nutmeg.

3. In another medium bowl, whisk together the eggs, sugar, oil, milk, and vanilla extract until well blended. Pour the wet ingredients into the dry and fold gently to combine. When the batter is smooth, transfer it to a piping bag fitted with a large round tip or a large plastic zip-top bag (once the batter is in the bag, work it to one side, and snip off the corner with scissors).

4. Pipe about a quarter of the batter into the doughnut pan (the batter should come about halfway up the sides of each well). Sprinkle half the apple pieces over the batter. Top off each well with more batter, filling to about ¼ inch from the top.

5. Bake until a toothpick comes out clean and the doughnuts are deeply golden around the edges, about 12 minutes. Let cool on a wire rack for 3 minutes before inverting the pan and tapping the doughnuts out onto the rack to cool.

6. Repeat the process with the second half of the batter and apple bits. These doughnuts are best served soon after baking.

Blueberry Maple Oatmeal Muffins

MAKES 1 DOZEN MUFFINS

Muffins are the world's most perfect food for a crazy grab-and-go lifestyle. But we've all heard the horror stories of muffins that are really more of a cupcake than anything resembling a decent breakfast when you do the nutritional breakdown. These babies, though, are like a cross between a good bowl of oatmeal and a hearty stack of whole-grain pancakes.

1¼ cups (10⅝ ounces/301 grams) well-shaken buttermilk

½ cup (6 ounces/168 grams) pure maple syrup

5 tablespoons (2½ ounces/71 grams) unsalted butter, melted and cooled

1 large egg

1 teaspoon pure vanilla extract

1⅓ cups (4¾ ounces/135 grams) old-fashioned rolled oats

1 cup plus 2 tablespoons (4¾ ounces/135 grams) whole wheat pastry flour, spooned and leveled

1 teaspoon baking soda

½ teaspoon fine sea salt

¼ teaspoon ground cinnamon

½ cup (2¾ ounces/78 grams) dried wild blueberries or raisins

Rolled oats and turbinado sugar, for sprinkling (optional)

1. In a large bowl, whisk together the buttermilk, maple syrup, butter, egg, and vanilla extract. Whisk in the oats. Set aside to soak for at least 45 minutes (or up to overnight in the refrigerator).

2. Position a rack in the center of the oven and preheat the oven to 425°F. Spray a 12-cup muffin tin with nonstick cooking spray.

3. In a medium bowl, whisk together the flour, baking powder, baking soda, salt, and cinnamon. Add the blueberries and stir them into the dry ingredients with your fingertips, breaking up any clumps of berries that may have formed.

4. When the oat mixture is finished soaking, gently fold in the dry ingredients with a flexible spatula, using as few strokes as possible to get the job done—it's better to see a few streaks of flour here and there than to risk overmixing.

TIP: *This batter must be made as soon as it's mixed. But! You can turn this recipe into a make-ahead wonder by whisking the wets and adding the oats to soak overnight in the fridge, and shaking the dry ingredients and berries together in a container with a tight-fitting lid. The next morning, all that's left to do is dump, stir, and bake.*

5. Using a standard-size ice cream scoop, portion the batter out into the prepared muffin tin. Sprinkle the tops with an extra bit of oats and sugar. Bake until the muffins are golden and a toothpick inserted in the center of the muffins comes out clean, about 15 minutes.

6. Let the muffins cool in the pan just for a minute or two until you can safely handle them, and tilt them out of their cups to cool. Serve slightly warm or at room temperature.

Homemade Fruit Leather

MAKES TEN 2¼ × 8½-INCH STRIPS

As a child of the eighties, I have a particular fondness for sheets of chewy, dehydrated fruit rolled up in cellophane. This homemade version allows me to pass on the legacy of that sweet, sticky lunch box finery to my own kids, while controlling the sweetener and the quality of the fruit in the final product. I recommend making double batches—this stuff tends to fly!

12 ounces (340 grams) very ripe fresh fruit, peeled and chopped✱

2 tablespoons (1½ ounces/42 grams) honey or agave nectar

1 teaspoon freshly squeezed lemon juice✱✱

✱ The best candidates for fruit leather are soft ones like berries and ripe stone fruit, as there's no need to cook the fruits first. Thawed, unsweetened frozen fruit works well here, too. Steam apples and pears in a bit of water until very soft, or you can even use store-bought unsweetened apple or pear sauce for a shortcut.

✱✱ To preserve the color of the fruit and prevent browning.

1. Position a rack in the center of the oven and preheat the oven to the lowest temperature that your oven will allow—ideally 170°F, but no more than 200°F. Line a large rimmed baking sheet, about 12 × 17 inches in size, with parchment paper.

2. In the bowl of a food processor fitted with a steel blade, combine the fruit, honey, and lemon juice. Process the fruit until you have a very smooth puree. If you're using berries with lots of little seeds, you can strain the puree, if you wish.

3. Pour the puree onto the prepared baking sheet. Use a small offset spatula to smooth the puree into a very thin, even layer—if you're using a 12 × 17-inch pan, the smoothed-out mixture will nearly fill the pan. Tilt and shimmy the pan a bit to even it out further.

4. Bake the fruit until it is dry to the touch all over with no tacky spots, anywhere from 2 to 5 hours depending on your oven's temperature. Let the fruit leather cool completely in the pan, and let it rest at room temperature for about 2 hours—the fruit leather will be almost brittle in spots when it first emerges from the oven, but a rest on the counter will allow it to soften.

5. Use a pair of kitchen scissors to cut through the fruit leather and the parchment, first cutting the sheet width-wise into 2 rectangles, then cutting each rectangle into five 2¼ × 8½-inch strips.

6. Roll up the cut pieces of fruit leather with the parchment on the outside, securing them with a length of twine. Store in an airtight container at room temperature for up to 1 month.

TIP: *Although this recipe begs to be customized with whatever tasty bits you love, don't skip the chia seeds—they actually help bind the treats!*

Chocolate Chip Oatmeal Raisin Treats

MAKES ABOUT FORTY 1-INCH BALLS

If you're looking for a homemade treat that will make you the queen of the playground set or something wholesome to stash in your bag for those midday slumps, look no further. This formula manages to take a whole bunch of superfoods and turn them into something that walks the line between an energy bar and a ball of cookie dough.

Once you've got the dates, oats, and chia seeds in the mix, there are about a million ways to riff on these treats. Use the volume of raisins as your guide for swapping in amounts of other, similar ingredients. Adding a handful of chopped dried apples for an apple-cinnamon kind of thing would be excellent. Or dried cranberries and a little white chocolate. Dried blueberries and lemon zest! I could go on. It's pretty hard to mess this one up.

1 cup (7 ounces/200 grams) pitted Medjool dates, tightly packed

1¾ cups (6⅛ ounces/175 grams) old-fashioned rolled oats

¾ cup (4¼ ounces/120 grams) raisins

⅓ cup (2 ounces/57 grams) bittersweet chocolate chips (60% to 70% cacao)

1 generous tablespoon (¾ ounce/21 grams) natural peanut, almond, or sunflower seed butter

1 teaspoon chia seeds

½ teaspoon ground cinnamon

¾ teaspoon pure vanilla extract

⅛ teaspoon fine sea salt

1. Place the dates in a medium bowl. Fill the bowl with hot water to cover the dates by about an inch. Let stand for 10 minutes. Drain.

2. In the bowl of a food processor, combine all the ingredients. Process continuously until the mixture comes together, forming a dough of sorts. You want the oats to be pretty much completely broken down, with a few bits of raisins and little chips of chocolate still visible.

3. Using a teaspoon-size scoop, portion out small pieces of dough, using your hands to roll them into balls about 1 inch in diameter. Place the balls on a cookie sheet. Chill until firm, about 30 minutes. Once chilled, transfer to an airtight container to store in the fridge for up to 10 days.

TIP: *This recipe uses a slightly different kind of date paste than the one listed on page 55. We want our dates to be nice and tacky here, more like a delicious edible "glue" than a soft fruit puree, so we're not soaking them quite as long as we would for baked goods. I like Medjool dates specifically for this recipe because they're extra sticky, but Deglet Noor dates work, too—they just require about 10 minutes' more soaking time.*

Coconut Cashews

MAKES ABOUT 3½ CUPS

As splendid as these caramelized, savory, crunchy cashews are as a daytime pick-me-up, I would be doing you a disservice if I didn't promote them as an even better cocktail accompaniment. I like to use lots of flaky sea salt to finish them off, and I adjust the amount of cayenne to fit the occasion and the palates of those who will be eating them.

1 large egg white

¼ teaspoon fine sea salt

¼ cup plus 1 tablespoon (1⅝ ounces/47 grams) coconut sugar

½ teaspoon ground cardamom

⅛ teaspoon cayenne pepper, or more to taste

2½ cups (12½ ounces/354 grams) raw cashews

6 tablespoons (1⅛ ounces/32 grams) unsweetened shredded coconut

¼ teaspoon flaky sea salt (such as Maldon)

1. Position a rack in the center of the oven and preheat the oven to 300°F. Line a rimmed baking sheet with parchment paper.

2. In a medium bowl, vigorously whisk together the egg white and salt for about 1 minute, or until an opaque white foam forms that barely holds a shape. Whisk in ¼ cup of the coconut sugar, the cardamom, and cayenne until the mixture is smooth and thick and the sugar has dissolved, about 1 minute more. Using a large flexible spatula, fold in the raw cashews and half of the shredded coconut until evenly coated. Turn the mixture out onto the prepared baking sheet and spread into an even layer. Sprinkle the flaky sea salt on top.

3. Bake the cashews for 15 minutes. Meanwhile, in a small bowl, combine the remaining 3 tablespoons shredded coconut and 1 tablespoon coconut sugar. After the first 15 minutes of baking time, quickly pull the pan from the oven and use a large spatula to gently stir and flip the cashews. Scatter the coconut–coconut sugar mixture over the cashews and return the pan to the oven. Bake for 15 minutes more, or until the cashews are golden and the coating is dry and crisp. Sprinkle on a bit more flaky sea salt, if desired, and let the cashews cool completely before serving or storing in an airtight container for up to 2 weeks.

Coconut Sugar: the femme fatale

Weight: 1 cup/5¼ ounces/150 grams

Characteristics: Exotic, alluring; you have to treat her just right or she can get a little volatile. Coconut sugar's flavor profile is totally unique—a wonderfully toasty, deeply caramelized, almost savory vibe. As this sugar doesn't come from actual coconuts, there is no coconutty flavor to be found here, so coconut phobics can relax and enjoy.

Where it comes from: Coconut sugar, sometimes also labeled coconut palm sugar, is the dried and granulated sap of flower buds from the coconut palm tree. Coconut palms are grown, and coconut sugar harvested, in many Southeast Asian countries, including Thailand, Indonesia, and the Philippines. It's easy to confuse coconut sugar or coconut palm sugar with straight-up palm sugar, which comes from different varieties of palm trees, such as sugar palms or date palms, which yield a much different sugar. So it's important to read the label closely to make sure you're getting the coconut sugar you're really after.

Best uses: Although coconut sugar can be used 1:1 for white granulated sugar in recipes (with a little loss of sweetness), there are definitely some applications that are better suited to coconut sugar than others. Coconut sugar tends to be drying, so I love it in things that have lots of fat or moisture, or in fruit purees, like banana, to compensate (check out the divine Coconut Sugar Banana Sheet Cake with Caramelized Coconut Sugar Frosting on page 95). Muffins, quick breads, and "soft baked"–style cookies tend to do well with coconut sugar.

Candies like toffees and caramels also take a seriously delicious turn when coconut sugar is in the mix. When it comes to candymaking, though, stick to candies that are in the soft-ball to soft-crack stage, such as the Orange Blossom Honey and Walnut Toffee on page 146—coconut sugar has a lower burning point than white sugar and can quickly burn and taste horribly acrid when it's cooked higher than 285°F.

Bonus points: Although spendy, coconut sugar is minimally processed and is considered a low-glycemic-index sweetener, which is making it a bit of a darling in the health food world. Because it's a minimally processed product, coconut sugar also has a good handful of retained nutrients going for it, such as magnesium, potassium, zinc, iron, B vitamins, and amino acids.

How to store: Coconut sugar tends to clump up, so to protect your investment, once you open the bag transfer the sugar to a tight-sealing container and keep it in a cool, dry place.

Sunflower Seed Nuggets

MAKES ABOUT 2 DOZEN 1½-INCH COOKIES

These little cookies aren't lookers, but they're perfect for when you want to whip up a little something for the sweet tooth that's on the virtuous side. Crisp on the outside, tender on the inside, with lots of toasty, sweet flavor, they also make a fine purse snack for when you need a little energy boost without the sugar crash, and they are gluten- and nut-free, too. They also couldn't be faster or simpler to make. Hooray!

1½ cups (7⅜ ounces/210 grams) roasted and unsalted sunflower seeds✶

¾ cup plus 2 tablespoons (4⅝ ounces/132 grams) coconut sugar

¼ teaspoon fine sea salt

2 large egg whites

¼ teaspoon pure vanilla extract

✶ Sometimes it can be tough to find roasted sunflower seeds that are unsalted, so if you have only roasted and salted seeds, just omit the additional salt in the recipe. If you have raw seeds, give them a quick toasting for a few minutes on a dry baking sheet as the oven preheats.

1. Position the racks in the upper and lower thirds of the oven and preheat the oven to 350°F. Line 2 baking sheets with parchment paper or silicone baking mats.

2. In the bowl of a food processor fitted with the steel blade, combine 1⅓ cups of the sunflower seeds, the sugar, and salt. Process until the seeds are ground into a flour, about 1 minute. Add the egg whites and vanilla extract and process until the batter is well blended, about 1 minute more. Chill the dough for 1 hour.

3. Using a small ice cream scoop or 2 spoons, drop the batter by teaspoonfuls onto the prepared baking sheet, 1 dozen per sheet. Sprinkle the remaining few tablespoons of sunflower seeds over the tops of the cookies. Bake until the cookies are a bit puffed, slightly cracked, and shiny on their surfaces, but still a bit soft if you press on their centers, 15 to 20 minutes. Let the cookies cool on the sheets for 5 minutes before using a thin spatula to transfer them to a wire rack to cool completely.

Little Plum, Walnut, and Maple Cakes

MAKES EIGHT 2½-INCH CAKES

In these humble tea cakes with huge flavor, the combination of juicy plums, walnuts, and maple is a favorite, but you can use a wonderfully wide spectrum of ingredients here. I love to nestle in a fresh fig half if figs are in season or switch up the fruit and nut combinations. Think almonds and apricots, pear and hazelnuts, raspberry and pistachio, peach and pecan for a little Southern flair. It's really fun to play with this one.

PREPARING THE PAN

1 tablespoon unsalted butter, very soft

2 tablespoons (⅞ ounce/23 grams) maple sugar

CAKES

1 cup (4 ounces/113 grams) chopped walnuts

⅓ cup (2⅛ ounces/61 grams) maple sugar

⅓ cup (1⅜ ounces/40 grams) whole wheat pastry flour, spooned and leveled

½ teaspoon pure vanilla extract

½ teaspoon ground cinnamon

¼ teaspoon fine sea salt

5 tablespoons (2½ ounces/71 grams) unsalted butter, browned and cooled (see page 75)

3 large egg whites, at room temperature

2 medium plums (each about 2¼ inches in diameter), cut into sixths, or 4 small Italian prune plums, halved*

1. Position a rack in the center of the oven and preheat the oven to 400°F.

2. Prepare the pan: Using your fingertips or a pastry brush, generously grease just 8 wells of a 12-cup muffin tin with the butter. Spoon about ¾ teaspoon of the maple sugar into each well. Slowly rotate the pan to create an even crust of sugar in the inside of each cup. Set the pan in the freezer to chill.

3. Make the cakes: In the bowl of a food processor fitted with the steel blade, combine the walnuts, maple sugar, flour, vanilla extract, cinnamon, and salt. Process just until the nuts are very finely ground. Add the browned butter and pulse several times until the mixture resembles wet sand.

*Italian prune plums are of a charmingly teeny size and perfect for fitting into these little cakes, but their season is fleeting, so I often end up using larger red plums cut into sixths. Of course, you'll have 4 wedges left over—baker's treat!

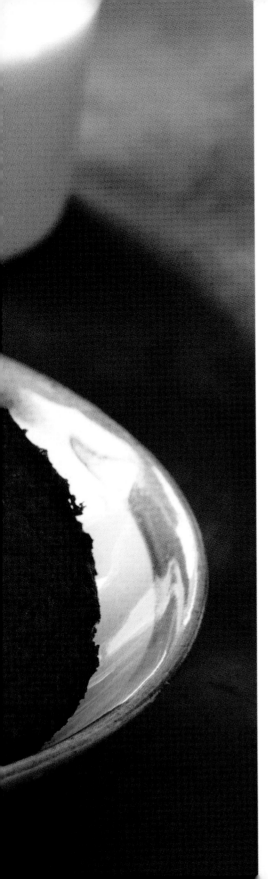

4. In a medium bowl, using a balloon whisk and an energetic arm or a handheld electric mixer, beat the egg whites to very soft peaks, like thickened cream that's barely whipped.

5. Add about a third of the whipped whites to the processor and pulse a few times to blend. Scrape the walnut batter into the bowl with the whites and fold gently to blend (it will look a mess at first, but keep folding gently and it will eventually come together and smooth out).

6. Remove the pan from the freezer and spoon the batter into the cups, about 3 tablespoons into each well. Press a wedge of plum in each cup, sinking them just a bit into the batter. Bake until the cakes are puffed, deeply browned around the edges, and any juice from the fruit is bubbling, 25 to 30 minutes. Let the cakes cool completely in the pan before loosening the edges with a thin metal spatula and turning them out of the pan.

TIP: *Maple sugar is basically evaporated maple syrup, so it has major flavor along with the nutrients of pure maple syrup. It's a bit spendy for everyday use, so I order it online for the best price and save it for recipes like this, where its unique flavor can really shine. See page 238 for more.*

Homemade Graham Crackers

MAKES ABOUT 3 DOZEN 2½-INCH CRACKERS

With small children in our household, graham crackers are akin to currency. With a box always stationed in the pantry, it was only a matter of time before I started playing with a homemade version. You can eat these straight up or in any recipe that calls for graham crackers, like the Nutty Graham Crust on page 240.

2¼ cups (9½ ounces/270 grams) whole wheat pastry flour, spooned and leveled

½ cup (4 ounces/113 grams) firmly packed light or dark muscovado sugar

1 teaspoon baking soda

½ teaspoon fine sea salt

½ cup (1 stick/4 ounces/113 grams) cold unsalted butter, cut into ¼-inch pieces

6 tablespoons (4½ ounces/126 grams) honey

1 tablespoon whole milk

1 teaspoon pure vanilla extract

CINNAMON GRAHAMS

In a small bowl, combine ¼ cup turbinado sugar or evaporated cane juice with 1 teaspoon ground cinnamon. Sprinkle all over the crackers before baking.

1. Position the racks in the upper and lower thirds of the oven and preheat the oven to 350°F. Line 2 baking sheets with parchment paper.

2. In the bowl of a food processor fitted with a steel blade, pulse together the flour, sugar, baking soda, and salt several times to combine. Sprinkle the butter over the dry ingredients. Pulse until the butter is broken down into pieces about the size of popcorn kernels, about 25 pulses.

3. In a small bowl, whisk together the honey, milk, and vanilla extract. Pour the mixture into the processor. Blend until a smooth dough forms.

4. Line a work surface with a large sheet of plastic wrap. Scrape out the dough onto the plastic. Pat the dough into a disk and wrap tightly. Chill in the refrigerator until the dough is very firm, at least 2 hours.

5. Lightly flour a work surface. Unwrap the dough and divide it in half. Rewrap and chill one-half. Working with one-half of the dough at a time, lightly flour a rolling pin and roll out the dough to a thickness of ⅛ inch. Use a pizza cutter or thin, sharp knife to cut 2-inch squares,

or use a cookie cutter to cut shapes. Place the cut crackers on the prepared baking sheets as you work. Gather, reroll, and cut the scraps.

6. Bake until firm on the edges and an even golden color, 14 to 16 minutes. During baking, the crackers will poof up, then deflate and start to crisp up during the last few minutes—they may still be a touch soft in the centers but will firm upon cooling. Transfer the crackers to a wire rack to cool completely. Repeat the rolling, cutting, and baking process with the remaining dough.

Figgy Graham Cups

MAKES ABOUT 20 GRAHAM CUPS

These baby cakes make for a perfect lunch box sweet. Even just one or two tucked into the box seem like a special treat, since there's so much packed into each bite—a chewy, almost blondie-like graham mini-muffin, a surprise chocolate center, and a dab of fig jam that brings to mind those iconic, chewy fig and wheat cookies from the supermarket.

For the grahams in this recipe, I prefer high-quality, store-bought crackers (like Mi-Del brand, which is made with only honey and molasses). I absolutely love the simple kitsch factor of this recipe—taking something readymade and transforming it into something else entirely. You can even swap out the homemade fig jam for ⅔ cup of low-sugar jarred preserves. So crafty!

FIG JAM

3 ounces (85 grams) dried black Mission figs, stemmed

⅓ cup (2⅝ ounces/75 grams) water

2 tablespoons (1½ ounces/43 grams) pure maple syrup

1 teaspoon freshly squeezed lemon juice

Pinch of fine sea salt

GRAHAM CUPS

12 full sheets (6¾ ounces/192 grams) honey-sweetened graham crackers, such as Mi-Del brand

¼ teaspoon baking powder

¼ teaspoon fine sea salt

¼ cup (3 ounces/84 grams) pure maple syrup

3 tablespoons (1½ ounces/43 grams) firmly packed dark muscovado sugar

1 large egg

½ teaspoon pure vanilla extract

3 tablespoons (1½ ounces/43 grams) unsalted butter, melted and cooled

1½ ounces (43 grams) bittersweet chocolate (60% to 70% cacao), cut into scant ½-inch chunks

1. Position a rack in the center of the oven and preheat the oven to 350°F. Grease 20 wells of a 24-cup mini-muffin tin with butter or nonstick cooking spray.

2. Make the fig jam: In a small saucepan, combine the figs, water, maple syrup, lemon juice, and salt. Set the pan over medium heat and bring the liquid to a boil. Reduce the heat to medium-low, partially cover the pot, and simmer until the figs are soft and the liquid has reduced by a third, about 8 minutes. Remove the pan from the heat, cover the pot completely, and let cool for about 5 minutes. Pour the figs and all the cooking liquid into a food processor fitted with a steel blade. Puree until nearly smooth. Transfer the jam to a small bowl. Rinse and dry the processor bowl and blade and fit both back onto the machine.

3. Make the graham cups: Place the graham crackers in the food processor and grind them to fine crumbs. Add the baking powder and salt and pulse a few times to blend. Dump the crumbs into a large mixing bowl.

4. Pour the maple syrup into the food processor. Add the sugar, egg, and vanilla extract. Puree for 1 full minute, or until smooth. With the processor running, stream in the butter. Blend until the mixture is lighter in color and aerated, about 1 minute more.

5. Pour the wet ingredients into the graham cracker crumbs. With a large, flexible spatula, gently fold the batter until evenly moistened. Use a small ice cream scoop or 2 spoons to portion the batter into the prepared tin, filling each well about halfway—1 scant tablespoon of batter per cup.

6. Gently press 1 chocolate chunk into the center of each portion of batter. Spoon ½ teaspoon of fig jam on top of each chocolate chunk. Bake until the graham cups are slightly puffed and golden and a toothpick inserted into the cakey part just to the side of the fig jam comes out clean, 12 to 14 minutes. Rotate the pan 180 degrees halfway through the baking.

7. Cool the graham cups in the pan set on a wire rack for about 5 minutes. While still warm, use a thin knife to loosen the edges of the cakes before nudging them out of the pan and letting them cool completely. Store in an airtight container at room temperature for up to 5 days.

Fake-Out Caramel Dip

MAKES ABOUT 1 CUP

Now let's not get crazy—as a bona fide caramel addict, I will tell you that nothing is quite like the real thing. But believe me when I say that this magical combination of dates, nut butter, and salt is surprisingly satisfying as a caramel dip stand-in. Not to mention a surefire, whole foods way to encourage a ridiculous level of sliced fruit consumption.

¾ cup (6 ounces/170 grams) Date Paste (see page 55)

¼ cup (2¼ ounces/64 grams) natural, salted nut butter of your choosing (I like peanut and almond butters here)

¼ teaspoon fine sea salt (more or less, to taste)

¼ teaspoon pure vanilla extract

Whisk together all the ingredients until well blended, or for a super-smooth dip, combine them in a food processor. Serve with sliced apples, pears, and bananas.

On Public Embarrassment and Date Paste

We all have a few slightly mortifying tales tucked away in our personal files. The kind of stories that make the hair on the back of your neck stand up just thinking about them, and yet, given a few cocktails and just the right party crowd, you might find yourself sharing one of them for a laugh. One of mine involves elbowing my way through a bustling produce section and approaching a busy grocery store employee, just as those super-noisy sprinkler thingies turned on over the lettuces, causing me to have to raise my voice to be heard.

"I'm looking for dates!" I bellowed, as several amused faces turned in my direction. Yeah. You can imagine the laughs, and the comments that followed, even fifteen minutes later, as a few other people made their way over to the butcher along the same shopping path as my own.

"Still looking for a date?" a leering old man asked me as I reached for the pork shoulder. No, sir. *No thank you at all.*

All uncomfortable life moments aside, I still stock up on dates at the grocery store (the dried-fruit variety, thankyouverymuch), because they're full of fruity sweetness and are wonderfully useful in baking. They're also a superfood, packing loads of fiber, iron, potassium, and B vitamins. Dates can be chopped up and stirred into batters and cookie doughs like raisins, or after a soak in hot water and a blitz in the food processor, they can become a powerhouse sweetener in place of white sugar, lending moisture and great flavor to the party as well.

When experimenting with date paste, start by trying 1 cup of date paste in place of 1 cup of white sugar in recipes like quick breads, muffins, and one-bowl cakes, and pull back on any additional liquid in the recipe by about 25 percent. There are several varieties of dates in markets these days, but I prefer the larger sticky Medjool or slightly smaller and drier Deglet Noor dates. Just be careful how you word your question when looking for them in stores.

Date Paste

MAKES ABOUT 3 CUPS (27 OUNCES/765 GRAMS)

3 cups (21 ounces/600 grams) lightly packed, pitted Medjool or Deglet Noor dates
3 cups (24 ounces/680 grams) boiling water

Place the dates in a large bowl. Pour the water over the dates. Cover the bowl tightly with plastic wrap and let soak—tender Medjool dates only need about 10 to 15 minutes to soak, while drier Deglet Noor dates can use a soak of about 1 hour. Drain the dates, reserving the soaking water. Place the dates in a food processor fitted with the steel blade. Process until the paste is very smooth, with few discernible bits of date skin in the mix. You're looking for a texture and thickness sort of like an airy peanut butter or apple butter—the paste should be very smooth, move freely in the processor, and not cling to the sides of the bowl. If it appears a little chunky or sticky, add a bit of the soaking water, just a teaspoon at a time to avoid making it too runny. Ultimately, the paste should be a medium caramel color, spoonable, and hold its shape when you scoop some out. Use the paste immediately, or store it in an airtight container in the refrigerator for up to 10 days.

Bonus: Date Syrup!

Don't pour that soaking liquid down the drain! It makes for the most divine liquid sweetener and makes you feel quite domestically accomplished—you know, waste not, want not and all of that.

Just pour the liquid into a medium saucepan, using a pot a little bigger than you think you'll need, as the liquid will bubble up really high as it's reducing. Place the pot over medium-high heat and boil the syrup, reducing it by about half. Strain it into a heatproof storage container (a mason jar works well), and let it cool before capping it and storing it in the fridge for up to 1 month.

Use the syrup anywhere you'd use a drizzle of liquid sweetener like maple syrup or honey on the fly—in oatmeal, over pancakes, in salad dressings and marinades, in hot and cold drinks of all sorts, even in cocktails in place of simple syrup.

Oat Jacks

MAKES 1 DOZEN 2½-INCH JACKS

When my son was a newborn, he wouldn't sleep unless he was in motion. And not just a gentle rocking—no, it had to be in the car, traveling at least 50 miles per hour to lull him to sleep (you couldn't tell me differently about that speed—mothers of newborns are like scientists this way). So most afternoons I could be found aimlessly cruising the freeways of the Bay Area like a deranged Sandy Bullock, desperate for him to finally crash.

During one of these involuntary road trips, I found myself starving and delirious with exhaustion and low blood sugar, but unable to stop the car, lest I wake the ticking time bomb in the backseat. After several drive-thru lines were deemed too long, I came upon a random coffee shop with a drive-up window, and placed my order in a hushed tone, applying and releasing the brake, asking for "any food you have that might be sort of healthy, but I don't really care." In return, I was given something called an oat jack. Chewy, slightly sweet, and packed with oats, nuts, and seeds, it was the ultimate in portable, edible sanity. It quite possibly saved my life that day. And now I pass my version of it on to you.

2 cups (7 ounces/200 grams) old-fashioned rolled oats

½ cup (3½ ounces/100 grams) pitted Medjool dates (about 5 large)

⅓ cup (1 ounce/28 grams) unsweetened shredded coconut

⅓ cup (1½ ounces/43 grams) pepitas (raw pumpkin seeds)

¼ cup (1½ ounces/43 grams) raisins

¼ cup (1¼ ounces/43 grams) roasted, salted sunflower seeds

¼ teaspoon ground cinnamon

½ cup (6 ounces/168 grams) brown rice syrup or honey*****

⅓ cup (2⅝ ounces/75 grams) coconut, grapeseed, or canola oil

¼ cup (1⅝ ounces/47 grams) rapadura, turbinado, or coconut sugar

½ teaspoon fine sea salt

½ teaspoon pure vanilla extract

TIP: *Made with brown rice syrup and gluten-free oats, these are vegan and gluten-free!*

* Both contribute moisture and chew but with varying degrees of sweetness. Honey will give you sweeter jacks.

1. Position a rack in the center of the oven and preheat the oven to 350°F. Line a 12-cup muffin tin with paper liners.

2. Place 1 cup of the oats into a large mixing bowl. In the bowl of a food processor fitted with the steel blade, grind the remaining 1 cup of oats to a flour (a few tweedy bits left in the mix is fine). Dump the oat flour into the mixing bowl. Add the dates to the processor and pulse until the dates are very finely chopped and start to cling together. Scrape the chopped dates into the bowl with the oats.

3. Add the coconut, pepitas, raisins, sunflower seeds, and cinnamon into the mixing bowl. Stir the mixture with your fingertips so that the oat flour helps to de-clump the dates.

4. In a small saucepan, combine the brown rice syrup, oil, rapadura, and salt. Place the pan over medium heat and stir gently, letting the syrup warm slowly. Do not let the syrup boil—heat it just to a bare simmer until the rapadura dissolves (if the syrup threatens to boil, lower the heat). Remove the pan from the heat. Stir in the vanilla extract.

5. Pour the syrup into the mixing bowl. With a large heatproof spatula, stir the dough until it's evenly moistened with no dry pockets. Use a standard ice cream scoop to portion the dough into the muffin cups, a level ¼ cup per oat jack.

6. Bake until lightly golden, 25 to 30 minutes. Don't overbake, or you'll toughen the jacks. Let cool completely in the pan on a wire rack.

TIP: *While good as soon as the jacks have cooled completely, the texture and flavor are even better the next day. The jacks can also be tightly wrapped and frozen for up to 1 month.*

Bake Sales and Edible Gifts

IN SPITE OF THE FACT that our modern lives seem to zoom along at 500 miles per hour, it's comforting to know that there are still plenty of opportunities to offer up something sweet and handmade. But for me, this all too often involves an opportunity that spooks me and sends me into a tailspin. Examples include the bake sale I forgot I signed up for; another friend just had a baby and deserves major comfort food; it's December 23, and I really should leave a little something for the mailman who hauls all those packages up my front steps. In these situations, I'm grateful for an arsenal of simple, sturdy treats for the sweet tooth that are perfect for wrapping up in festive ways. And with natural sugars in the mix, you get stepped-up familiar favorites that wow every time.

TIP: *I've been known to eat these little babies frozen.*

Dark, Fudgy Muscovado Brownies

MAKES TWENTY-FIVE 1½-INCH SQUARES

Dark muscovado sugar pulls double duty in this insanely rich, fudgy brownie—the sugar's deep molasses flavor marries fabulously with bittersweet chocolate, and its moist quality (along with a gooey hit of brown rice syrup) contributes a chocolate-truffle-esque chew. If there ever was a mysterious "bad boy" version of a brownie, this would be it.

6 tablespoons (3 ounces/84 grams) unsalted butter

6 ounces (168 grams) bittersweet chocolate (60% to 70% cacao), chopped

3 tablespoons (⅝ ounce/18 grams) unsweetened natural cocoa powder

¾ cup (6 ounces/168 grams) firmly packed dark muscovado sugar

3 tablespoons (2¼ ounces/63 grams) brown rice syrup

2 teaspoons pure vanilla extract

½ teaspoon fine sea salt

2 large eggs, cold

½ cup (2⅛ ounces/60 grams) whole wheat pastry flour, spooned and leveled

TIP: *Using a plastic knife—the humble, disposable kind used for picnics—makes for the cleanest-edged brownies you've ever seen.*

1. Position a rack in the center of the oven and preheat the oven to 350°F. Line an 8 × 8-inch metal baking pan with an 8-inch-wide strip of aluminum foil or parchment paper, leaving a few inches of overhang on 2 sides. Lightly grease the pan with nonstick cooking spray or butter.

2. In a large heatproof bowl, melt the butter and chocolate together in the microwave with 60-second bursts of high power, stirring well after each interval until smooth. Whisk in the cocoa powder. Whisk in the sugar, brown rice syrup, vanilla extract, and salt until well blended (a few small lumps of sugar may remain—the rough charm of dark muscovado!). Whisk in the eggs one at a time. Switch from a whisk to a spatula and add the flour, stirring gently just until no traces of flour remain. Set the batter aside to rest for 10 minutes. Scrape the batter into the prepared pan and smooth the top.

3. Bake until a toothpick inserted in the center comes out mostly clean, with a smudge of chocolate at the end, and the brownie slab has just begun to pull away from the sides of the pan, about 30 minutes. Cool completely in the pan on a wire rack. Remove the brownies using the foil or parchment "handles" and transfer to a cutting board. Cut into squares. Refrigerate in an airtight container for up to 5 days.

Toasted Coconut-Almond Meringue Bark

MAKES ABOUT 2 DOZEN 2-INCH SHARDS

If you're as in love with airy, sweet, crunchy meringue as I am, you'll love this twist on meringue cookies. It's basically a lazy meringue lover's dream, no piping or scooping of little mounds required. These shingles of sugary bliss are laced with the tropical flavors of light muscovado sugar, coconut, and dark rum.

This recipe is pictured on page 65.

¾ cup (2⅛ ounces/60 grams) unsweetened shredded coconut*

½ cup (2⅛ ounces/60 grams) sliced almonds

2 large egg whites

⅛ teaspoon fine sea salt

⅓ cup (2¼ ounces/71 grams) firmly packed light muscovado sugar

1 teaspoon cornstarch

1 teaspoon dark rum (such as Myers's)

½ teaspoon pure vanilla extract

*Sometimes labeled "desiccated" coconut.

1. Position an oven rack in the center of the oven and preheat the oven to 350°F.

2. On a large rimmed baking sheet, toss together the coconut and almonds and spread into an even layer (really give the coconut and nuts lots of room to dry and toast—use all the space on the sheet!). Bake until crisp and lightly golden, stirring occasionally, 8 to 10 minutes. Transfer the toasted coconut and almonds to a plate to cool completely.

3. Wipe the sheet tray clean with a paper towel and line it with parchment paper. Lower the oven temperature to 225°F.

4. Into the bowl of an electric mixer fitted with the whisk attachment, pour the egg whites and salt. Beat on medium-high speed until soft peaks form, about 3 minutes. Meanwhile, in a small bowl, work together the sugar and cornstarch with your fingertips until the sugar is lump-free and appears drier in texture.

5. Once the egg whites have reached soft peaks, gradually add the sugar to the whipping whites. Once all the sugar has been added, raise the mixer speed to high and whip until the meringue is stiff and glossy, about 3 minutes more.

6. Fold three-quarters of the cooled coconut and almonds into the meringue. Spread the meringue out onto the prepared baking sheet into a rough, 8 × 12-inch rectangle, about ⅓ inch thick. Sprinkle the remaining coconut and almonds evenly over the top.

7. Bake until the meringue is dry and crisp, about 1½ hours. Let the meringue cool completely on the baking sheet set over a wire rack. Break into pieces. Store in an airtight container at room temperature in a very cool, dry place for up to 2 weeks.

Next-Level Chocolate Chip Cookies

MAKES 2 DOZEN 3-INCH COOKIES

This cookie represents everything I love about baking with natural sugars. It's a comfort food classic with a major boost in the taste and texture department, a great depth of molasses flavor from the dark muscovado sugar, and a sweet crunch throughout from coarse turbinado. I use whole wheat pastry flour because I find its nuttiness is a perfect fit here, but you could also use all-purpose or a half-and-half mix of both.

1⅔ cup (7 ounces/200 grams) whole wheat pastry flour, spooned and leveled

½ teaspoon fine sea salt

½ teaspoon baking soda

¼ teaspoon baking powder

½ cup (1 stick/4 ounces/113 grams) unsalted butter, at room temperature

⅔ cup (5¼ ounces/148 grams) firmly packed dark muscovado sugar

½ cup (3½ ounces/100 grams) turbinado sugar

2 teaspoons pure vanilla extract

1 large egg, at room temperature

1 generous cup (7 ounces/200 grams) bittersweet chocolate chips (60% to 70% cacao)

1. In a medium bowl, whisk together the flour, salt, baking soda, and baking powder.

2. In the bowl of an electric mixer fitted with the paddle attachment, beat together the butter, sugars, and vanilla extract on medium-high speed for 5 full minutes, or until lightened in texture and color. Add the egg and beat 1 minute more. Reduce the speed to low and stir in the dry ingredients. Stir in the chocolate chips. Cover the bowl and chill the dough in the refrigerator for at least 1 hour or up to overnight.

3. When you're ready to bake, position the racks in the upper and lower thirds of the oven and preheat the oven to 350°F. Line 2 baking sheets with parchment paper.

4. Using a small ice cream scoop or 2 spoons, shape the dough into balls (2 tablespoons each) and arrange on the prepared baking sheets. Bake until the cookies are set enough on their perimeters so that you can lift the very edges with a fingertip, but still soft in the centers, 12 to 14 minutes—do not overbake. Let the cookies cool completely on the baking sheets.

Toasted Coconut–Almond
Meringue Bark
(page 62)

Next-Level
Chocolate Chip
Cookies
(page 64)

Mrs. Braun's
Oatmeal Cookies
(page 68)

Double Chocolate
Muscovado Cookies
(page 66)

Double Chocolate Muscovado Cookies

MAKES 4 DOZEN 2-INCH COOKIES

If you've been near a food magazine or website within the past several years, then you're probably familiar with the glory that is the World Peace Cookie, a recipe originally from the incomparable pastry chef Pierre Hermé, popularized by the wonderful baker and writer Dorie Greenspan. It's a perfect, sweet-salty, buttery little gem that has you carving a divot into your kitchen floor as you walk back and forth from the cookie jar.

I wanted to give that awesome cookie a natural-sugars spin, a World Peace Cookie 2.0 if you will, with even more chocolaty depth. This recipe bolsters the cocoa with the nuttiness of whole wheat pastry flour and browned butter and the dark richness of muscovado sugar.

This recipe is pictured on page 65.

1 cup plus 2 tablespoons (4¾ ounces/135 grams) whole wheat pastry flour, spooned and leveled

⅓ cup (1⅛ ounces/33 grams) unsweetened natural cocoa powder

½ teaspoon fine sea salt

½ cup (1 stick/4 ounces/113 grams) unsalted butter, browned and chilled (see page 75)

⅔ cup (5¼ ounces/150 grams) firmly packed dark muscovado sugar

1 teaspoon pure vanilla extract

1 large egg yolk

1 tablespoon whole milk

6 ounces (170 grams) bittersweet chocolate (60% to 70% cacao), chopped into ¼-inch bits

1. Into a medium bowl, sift together the flour, cocoa powder, and salt.

2. Scrape the solid browned butter (and all those tasty browned bits from the edges!) into the bowl of an electric mixer fitted with the paddle attachment. Add the sugar and vanilla extract. Beat on medium speed until fluffy and much lighter in color, about 3 minutes—the appearance will start out with the dark sugar dominating but over the beating time will transform into something looking like a brown-speckled buttercream frosting. Beat in the egg yolk, then the milk.

3. Reduce the mixer speed to the lowest setting and stir in the dry ingredients. Stir in the chocolate bits and mix until the dough first comes together and then pulls off the sides of the bowl in 3 or 4 large sections, about 1 minute. Gather the sections and divide the dough in half. Line a work surface with a sheet of plastic wrap. Form half the dough into a log about 7 inches long and 1¼ inches

in diameter, using the plastic wrap to help you form it. Wrap the dough log tightly. Shape and wrap the second half of the dough. Chill in the refrigerator until very firm, about 3 hours.

4. When you're ready to bake, position the racks in the upper and lower thirds of the oven and preheat the oven to 325°F. Line 2 baking sheets with parchment paper.

5. Using a thin, sharp knife, slice each log of dough into twenty-four ¼-inch-thick cookies. Place the cookies on the prepared baking sheets, 2 dozen cookies per sheet. Bake until the edges are set, but the centers of the cookies are still very soft, about 12 minutes—don't overbake! They won't look done but will firm up as they cool. Let the cookies cool on the baking sheets set over wire racks. Store in an airtight container at room temperature for up to 5 days.

TIP: *The dough logs can be frozen for up to 6 months.*

Mrs. Braun's Oatmeal Cookies

MAKES ABOUT 2½ DOZEN 2¾-INCH COOKIES

This is a Real Sweet switch-up on one of my family's most beloved recipes.

This recipe is pictured on page 65.

1½ cups (5¼ ounces/150 grams) old-fashioned rolled oats

⅔ cup (2⅞ ounces/80 grams) whole wheat pastry flour, spooned and leveled

½ teaspoon baking soda

½ teaspoon fine sea salt

½ teaspoon ground cinnamon

½ cup (1 stick/4 ounces/113 grams) unsalted butter, at room temperature

½ cup (3½ ounces/100 grams) turbinado sugar

½ cup (3 ounces/85 grams) rapadura

2 large egg yolks

1 large whole egg

1 teaspoon pure vanilla extract

½ cup (2⅞ ounces/80 grams) golden raisins

½ cup (2 ounces/57 grams) pecans, toasted and chopped (see page 75)

1. In a medium bowl, whisk together the oats, flour, baking soda, salt, and cinnamon.

2. In the bowl of an electric mixer fitted with the paddle attachment, beat together the butter, sugar, and rapadura on medium speed until noticeably paler in color, about 5 minutes. Add the egg yolks, egg, and vanilla extract and beat until fluffy, about 1 minute more. Reduce the speed to low and stir in the dry ingredients until well blended. Stir in the raisins and pecans. Cover the bowl and chill the dough for at least 1 hour.

3. When you're ready to bake, position the oven racks in the upper and lower thirds of the oven and preheat the oven to 350°F. Line 2 baking sheets with parchment paper.

4. Using a small ice cream scoop or 2 spoons, drop the dough by tablespoonfuls onto the prepared baking sheets, 1 dozen per sheet (the cookies will spread during baking). Bake until deeply golden and set on the edges but still soft in the centers, about 15 minutes (rotate the sheets from top to bottom and front to back halfway through baking). Let the cookies cool on the baking sheets for about 5 minutes before using a thin metal spatula to remove them to a wire rack to cool completely. Store in an airtight container at room temperature for up to 5 days.

Muscovado: the bad boy

Weight: 1 cup/8 ounces/227 grams

Characteristics: Rich, heady, sticky, dark, rough, and unrefined. Think supermarket dark brown sugar on steroids. Light muscovado is much milder and comparable to supermarket dark brown sugar in color and flavor. Dark muscovado, on the other hand, is so shockingly dark and full of molasses flavor, it teeters on the edge of being bittersweet, with an almost savory quality.

Where it comes from: Sometimes labeled "Barbados," "moist," or "molasses sugar," muscovado sugar is a minimally processed sugar derived from sugarcane. It's made by boiling down sugarcane until it evaporates, leaving sticky crystals behind. Muscovado sugar isn't chemically treated or stripped of its molasses, which gives it its deep color and sticky texture. Most muscovado production happens on the islands of Barbados, Mauritius, and the Philippines, close to the sugarcane source, by people who have been producing the sugar for generations, making it a sort of heirloom sugar with great character. This is a sugar with a true sense of story in its rich flavor.

Best uses: Anywhere you'd use brown sugar, use an equal, firmly packed measure of muscovado. It's most impressive in baked goods where that alluring combination of crisp edges and chewy centers is the order of the day—think chewy cookies, brownies, bar cookies, and moist, dense, sticky cakes. Muscovado sugar is amazing paired with spices and chocolate, as in the Spiced Chocolate Molasses Buttons on page 83 and pumped-up candies like the Gingerbread Fudge on page 134. Tropical fruits such as bananas and pineapple (and perhaps a hit of dark rum?) are a slam dunk with muscovado.

Dark muscovado in particular can often have some hard clumps in it, so I often go for extra mixing time or run the sugar through a food processor. Sometimes I just go with its unrefined flow and enjoy bonus little molten sugary nuggets in my baked goods. To me, dark muscovado sugar is the ultimate "I can't put my finger on it, but something in this recipe is absolutely *incredible*" kind of ingredient.

Bonus points: Because it's minimally processed, muscovado sugar retains many of the benefits of sugarcane, which in its untouched state is actually a very nutrient-dense plant. Muscovado is rich in calcium, iron, magnesium, vitamins A and C, and lots of the B vitamins, and it has antioxidant properties.

How to store: Muscovado sugar can be tricky to find and expensive, so I buy it in bulk online for the best price and store it wisely. Keeping muscovado sugar moist is key. Since it's often shipped from exotic locales, your muscovado might come a bit dry, like a big brick. In that case, break it up as best as you can into a container with a tight-fitting lid and add a slice of bread or half an apple. Let the sealed container sit overnight, discard the bread or apple, and you'll have softer, scoopable muscovado sugar at the ready.

Chocolate Chip Cookie Brittle

ABOUT 3 DOZEN 3-INCH PIECES

Such a simple name for something so addictive. I've been making a white sugar version of this treat for years, but swapping in turbinado gives the whole thing a hint of brown sugar flavor without compromising crunch the way moist brown sugar would—and it makes the ultimate edible gift! You really, truly, can't eat just one piece of this stuff. It's as if you can feel it becoming part of your DNA as you crunch. Buttery, sugary, and a touch salty, studded with bits of bittersweet chocolate. Glorious.

14 tablespoons (7 ounces/200 grams) unsalted butter, cut into tablespoons

1 cup (7 ounces/200 grams) turbinado sugar

2 teaspoons pure vanilla extract

1 teaspoon fine sea salt

2 cups (9 ounces/256 grams) unbleached all-purpose flour

½ cup (2⅛ ounces/60 grams) finely chopped pecans or walnuts

¾ cup (4½ ounces/128 grams) bittersweet chocolate chips (60% to 70% cacao)

1. Position a rack in the center of the oven and preheat the oven to 350°F. Have ready a rimmed 12 × 17-inch baking sheet.

2. In a large heatproof bowl, combine the butter and sugar. Microwave on high power just until the butter is hot and almost completely melted and the sugar has begun to dissolve, about 2 minutes (alternatively, you can melt the butter and sugar together in a saucepan over medium heat, being careful not to bring the mixture to a boil).

3. Remove the bowl from the microwave (or the saucepan from the heat) and whisk until the butter is completely melted. Let cool for 5 minutes. Whisk again continuously for 1 minute, or until the mixture is thickened and smooth and no longer appears separated. Whisk in the vanilla extract and salt. Stir in the flour until well incorporated. Stir in half of the finely chopped nuts.

4. Turn out the dough onto the sheet pan and pat it into a very thin, even layer with your hands (it won't look as if you'll be able to fill the entire pan, but you will—just keep on patting and spreading out the dough all the way to the

edges of the pan). Use an offset spatula to give the dough a smooth finish. Sprinkle the chocolate chips and the remaining chopped nuts over the dough and press them lightly into it with your hands.

5. Bake for 22 to 25 minutes, or until light golden brown and slightly firm to the touch all over, rotating the pan 180 degrees every 7 to 8 minutes to encourage even baking. Let cool in the pan for 3 minutes. Line a second sheet pan with parchment paper. Flip the brittle slab onto the paper and then immediately invert it right side up onto a cooling rack, peeling off the parchment. Cool completely. Break into pieces. Store in an airtight container for up to 5 days.

Iced Muscovado Caramel-Nut Blondies

MAKES SIXTEEN 2-INCH BAR COOKIES

What's not to love about a rich, chewy blondie packed with brown sugar flavor and studded with toasty nuts? Add to that a slick of sweet-salty frosting that's based on those glorious, shiny, old-fashioned caramel icings, and I'd say we're in business.

BLONDIES

1 cup (4¼ ounces/120 grams) whole wheat pastry flour, spooned and leveled

¾ teaspoon baking powder

½ teaspoon fine sea salt

½ cup (1 stick/4 ounces/113 grams) unsalted butter, browned and slightly cooled (see page 75)

¾ cup (6 ounces/170 grams) firmly packed dark muscovado sugar

1 large egg

1 teaspoon pure vanilla extract

½ cup (2 ounces/57 grams) chopped, toasted pecans or walnuts (see page 79)

1. Position a rack in the center of the oven and preheat the oven to 350°F. Lightly grease an 8 × 8-inch square baking pan and line it with an 8-inch-wide strip of parchment paper or aluminum foil, long enough to leave a few inches of overhang on 2 opposite sides of the pan.

2. Make the blondies: Into a medium bowl, sift together the flour, baking powder, and salt.

3. In a large bowl, energetically whisk together the butter and sugar until the sugar has begun to absorb the butter and dissolve, about 2 minutes. Whisk in the egg and vanilla extract. Switch to a spatula and fold in the flour mixture until well blended. Fold in the pecans or walnuts. Spread the batter into the prepared pan and smooth the top. Bake until golden and set and a toothpick inserted into the center comes out clean, about 22 minutes—don't overbake them, or they'll dry out. Let cool completely in the pan set on a wire rack.

(Recipe continues on the next page.)

ICING

⅓ cup (2⅝ ounces/75 grams) firmly packed dark muscovado sugar

3 tablespoons (1½ ounces/43 grams) unsalted butter, cut into tablespoons

¼ teaspoon fine sea salt

2 tablespoons (1 ounce/28 grams) milk

¼ teaspoon pure vanilla extract

⅓ cup (1⅜ ounces/39 grams) organic confectioners' sugar

4. Make the icing: Combine the sugar, butter, and salt in a medium saucepan. Melt together over medium heat, stirring often with a heatproof spatula. Bring the mixture to a boil and stir in the milk. Boil for 2 minutes, stirring occasionally. Stir in the vanilla extract. Dump in the confectioners' sugar and stir the icing energetically for about 3 minutes, or until the icing is thickened and smooth, is beginning to lose some gloss, and is a touch lighter in color—more of a thin icing than a pourable glaze.

5. Top the blondies with the icing and spread it evenly with a spatula. Let the icing set in the refrigerator for 10 minutes before cutting and serving the blondies. Store in an airtight container for up to 4 days.

How to Brown Butter

Every once in a while, a kitchen technique comes along that sort of blows your head off your shoulders and changes up your routine forever. Like browning butter. Sure, we've all accidentally slipped a pat of butter into a too-hot skillet and seen it immediately turn into a freckled liquid that discolors our scrambled eggs. But when you brown butter *on purpose* and incorporate that nutty, toasty flavor into baked goods, it's really a next-level kind of thing.

There are a few components in butter: butterfat, milk solids, and water. When butter is melted and then allowed to continue to cook, the water eventually evaporates, leaving behind the butterfat and milk solids. Once their cushion of water is out of the picture, the milk solids get even hotter and begin to brown, sinking to the bottom of the pan. These deeply golden bits are what give browned butter its intoxicating fragrance and flavor (as long as you remove the pan from the heat before the nut-brown bits burn and turn bitter).

There are a few recipes in this book that call for browned butter, and it couldn't be simpler to make. Set a small saucepan or skillet over medium-high heat. Cut the amount of unsalted butter needed for the recipe into small chunks and place them in the pan. Melt the butter, and once it's completely melted, let it bubble and sizzle away for a couple of minutes, swirling the pan occasionally. Listen closely—once the sizzling starts to quiet down, that means that the water has evaporated, and the milk solids will begin to brown.

Swirl the pan and tip it from side to side to examine the color of the solids, and give the butter a good sniff. Pull the pan from the heat when the solids are a deep golden brown and the butter smells nutty and wonderful. The whole process of browning butter takes 5 to 7 minutes. Stop the browned butter from cooking further by immediately pouring it into a heatproof bowl to cool. When the butter is cooled, use it in any recipe that calls for melted butter.

You can also use browned butter in recipes that call for the butter to be in solid form, like frostings, cake batters, and cookie doughs. Simply pour the browned butter into a heatproof container (such as a small metal baking pan) and freeze for several minutes until the butter is completely firm. Scrape the solid browned butter out using a spoon, proceed with the recipe as usual, and then wait for people to swoon over your baked goods.

Oatmeal and Turbinado Cream Cookie Sandwiches

MAKES FIFTEEN 2½-INCH COOKIE SANDWICHES

Consider these babies a nod to those iconic packaged oatmeal cookie sandwiches of your youth, and give my regards to that darling Little Debbie, even though this version is infinitely better (sorry, Deb). The oatmeal cookies all by themselves are terrific; pairing them with a creamy turbinado sugar filling not only gilds the lily, but gives you a totally legitimate excuse to eat two cookies at the same time.

OATMEAL COOKIES

1½ cups (5¼ ounces/150 grams) old-fashioned rolled oats

1 cup (8 ounces/227 grams) firmly packed dark muscovado sugar

½ cup (4¼ ounces/120 grams) whole wheat pastry flour, spooned and leveled

½ teaspoon fine sea salt

½ teaspoon baking soda

¼ teaspoon baking powder

½ teaspoon ground cinnamon

¼ teaspoon freshly grated nutmeg

½ cup (1 stick/4 ounces/113 grams) cold unsalted butter, cut into cubes

1 large egg yolk*

*Save the egg white for the filling! (Filling ingredients follow on the next page.)

1. Make the cookies: In the bowl of a food processor fitted with the steel blade, grind the oats to a flour. Add the muscovado sugar, flour, salt, baking soda, baking powder, cinnamon, and nutmeg and process briefly to blend. Toss in the butter and process until the butter is well incorporated and the dough begins to clump and pull off the sides of the bowl. Add the egg yolk and pulse until the dough comes together with no dry pockets.

2. Line a work surface with a large sheet of plastic wrap. Turn out the dough onto the plastic wrap and form it into a log about 10 inches long and 1½ inches in diameter. Wrap the dough tightly. Chill the dough until firm, at least 3 hours in the refrigerator.

3. When you're ready to bake, position a rack in the center of the oven and preheat the oven to 350°F. Line 2 baking sheets with parchment paper. Use a thin, sharp knife to slice the dough log into 30 rounds, each about ⅓ inch thick. Transfer the rounds to the prepared baking sheets. Bake until golden and firm, about 15 minutes. Transfer the cookies to a wire rack to cool completely.

TURBINADO CREAM FILLING

⅔ cup (4⅝ ounces/132 grams) turbinado sugar

3 large egg whites

¼ teaspoon fine sea salt

½ cup (1 stick/4 ounces/113 grams) butter, cut into ½-inch cubes, soft but still cool

1 teaspoon pure vanilla extract

TIP: *If the filling isn't whipping into shape after a couple of minutes, the mixture may be too warm—pop the bowl into the freezer for a few minutes to chill it down and try whipping again.*

TIP: *For extra sparkle, add a rim of turbinado sugar to each cookie: Spread about ¼ cup of turbinado sugar on a small baking sheet. Whisk together 1 egg with a tablespoon of water. Lightly brush the egg wash all over the dough log, and roll the log through the sugar before slicing the dough into rounds.*

4. Make the filling: Combine the turbinado sugar, egg whites, and salt in the metal bowl of a stand mixer. Set the bowl over a pan of gently simmering water. Whisk until the mixture is slightly foamy and the sugar has completely dissolved—rub a bit of the mixture between your fingertips to make sure no coarse bits of sugar are lurking in the bottom of the bowl. Attach the bowl to the mixer fitted with a whisk attachment. Beat on high speed until the meringue is stiff and glossy and the bowl is cool to the touch, 8 to 10 minutes depending on your mixer.

5. Reduce the speed to medium and beat in the butter a tablespoon at a time, giving each knob of butter ample time to incorporate into the filling before adding the next. About the time that all the butter has been added, the filling will look like a curdled and separated mess and you might start to panic, but don't—it will come together with another minute or so of whipping time. When the filling is smooth, beat in the vanilla extract. (Hooray, you've just made Swiss meringue buttercream!)

6. To fill the cookies, either load the filling into a piping bag fitted with a large round tip or use a small scoop or 2 spoons. Flip half the cookies over and top each with 2 teaspoons of the filling. Sandwich with the remaining cookies and press gently to adhere. Store at room temperature for the first day, and refrigerate them for longer storage, up to 3 days.

How to Toast Nuts

I'm a sucker for a good baking booster, and toasting nuts and seeds before adding them to baked goods is one of the simplest. Even if you've got access to really fresh nuts and seeds, the flavor can still be a bit lacking. Toasting nuts allows their earthy, flavorful oils to be released and permeate a batter or dough, and it also makes the nuts or seeds crunchier for a nice added textural element. Sample two oatmeal cookies, one with toasted walnuts and one with untoasted, and you'll never go untoasted again.

Nuts and seeds can be toasted in a dry skillet on the stovetop, but you have to babysit them, watching and stirring often to prevent them from burning. Since I'm often doing a dozen things at once in the kitchen, as long as my oven is already preheating for a recipe I avoid the stovetop method (inevitably some small person comes wandering in, needing a snack and playing 20 Questions, while I'm measuring other ingredients and the mixer is whirring).

Instead, I like to toast nuts and seeds in the oven while it's preheating. It takes a little more time—8 to 10 minutes for nuts, 4 to 6 minutes for seeds, depending on the size of the pieces and the temperature of the oven—but it's a gentler approach than the stove and puts the heat of the oven to good use while it's waiting. Any metal baking pan and oven temperature from 350 to 400°F works fine for toasting; make sure to shake the pan every few minutes and check the progress. While they're still warm and a bit glossy with their oils, season the pieces with a pinch of fine sea salt, if you like—this makes a great crunchy, salty-sweet garnish for ice creams and puddings.

Just about any treat that calls for nuts and seeds to be mixed in can benefit from a pre-toasting, but there are a couple of exceptions. If a streusel or other exterior topping involves nuts, I leave them untoasted, as they tend to burn while being exposed to heat during a long bake. I also don't toast nuts and seeds that will be incorporated into high-heat candy like toffees and brittles. For that, I tend to use raw nuts, as the screaming-hot sugar will roast the nuts on contact, and if they're preroasted, they can become overcooked and bitter.

Crunchy Almond Shortbread

MAKES ABOUT 40 COOKIES

The best shortbread always has a bit of rice flour for an irresistible snappy, sandy texture. And because almond shortbread is divine, I thought I'd really bump up the nuttiness and use almond flour instead of wheat flour. Before I knew it, I had a wonderfully crisp, nutty shortbread on my hands that also happens to be gluten-free. High five!

For economy and the aesthetic of all those beautiful brown flecks of almond skin, this recipe starts by making your own almond flour with raw nuts. If you want to seek out something premade, you'll want to look for speckled "almond meal" rather than creamy white blanched almond flour, which is made from skinless almonds and therefore absorbs liquids differently.

1¼ cups (6¼ ounces/177 grams) raw almonds

⅔ cup (3¾ ounces/107 grams) white rice flour

⅔ cup (4⅝ ounces/132 grams) turbinado sugar

½ teaspoon fine sea salt

¼ teaspoon baking soda

10 tablespoons (5 ounces/142 grams) unsalted butter, at cool room temperature, cut into tablespoons

1 teaspoon pure vanilla extract

¼ teaspoon almond extract

1 large egg, lightly beaten

¾ cup (3¾ ounces/107 grams) almonds, toasted and coarsely chopped

TIP: *The dough planks can be frozen for up to 6 months.*

1. In the bowl of a food processor fitted with the steel blade, process the raw almonds to a flour, about 30 seconds. To the processor, add the rice flour, sugar, salt, and baking soda. Process until the sugar is broken down a bit, about 1 minute.

2. Scatter the butter over the top, and add the vanilla and almond extracts. Process just until the dough starts to come together and pull off the sides of the processor bowl. Add the egg and process to blend well. Toss in the toasted almonds and pulse until the dough is well blended and the almonds are chopped a bit finer.

3. Line a work surface with a large sheet of plastic wrap. Divide the dough in half and place half on the plastic wrap (the dough will be very soft). Shape the dough into a 2 × 6-inch plank that's about 1¼ inches thick. Wrap the plastic tightly around the dough plank. Shape and wrap the remaining dough. Chill in the refrigerator until very firm, about 4 hours.

4. When you're ready to bake, position a rack in the center of the oven and preheat the oven to 325°F. Line 2 baking sheets with parchment paper.

5. Slice each plank into twenty ⅓-inch-thick cookies. Evenly space the cookies on the prepared baking sheets, 20 to a sheet. Bake until golden and firm to the touch all over, 20 to 25 minutes.

6. Let the cookies cool on the sheets for 5 minutes before transferring to wire racks to cool completely (they will be quite fragile right out of the oven, so be sure to give them a rest before transferring them to the cooling racks). Store in an airtight container at room temperature for up to 5 days.

TIP: *To glitz up your shortbread, thoroughly beat 1 additional egg with 1 tablespoon of water. With a pastry brush, paint the egg wash all over the chilled dough planks, then coat them in turbinado sugar before slicing into cookies.*

Spiced Chocolate Molasses Buttons

MAKES ABOUT 4 DOZEN COOKIES

These make a great holiday cookie—a hit with the chocolate lovers, the spice cookie lovers, and those who are drawn to the prettiest of the cookie tin contenders. This cookie gets a double hit of raw sugars: sticky dark muscovado in the dough and a roll through turbinado sugar that adds crunch and a naturally glittering finish around a puddle of bittersweet chocolate ganache.

COOKIES

1½ cups plus 2 tablespoons (5⅛ ounces/144 grams) unbleached all-purpose flour, spooned and leveled

6 tablespoons (1¼ ounces/36 grams) unsweetened natural cocoa powder

¾ teaspoon ground cinnamon

½ teaspoon ground ginger

⅛ teaspoon allspice

¾ teaspoon baking soda

½ teaspoon fine sea salt

10 tablespoons (5 ounces/142 grams) unsalted butter, at room temperature

½ cup (4 ounces/113 grams) firmly packed dark muscovado sugar

1 teaspoon pure vanilla extract

1 large egg

¼ cup (3 ounces/84 grams) unsulphured molasses

½ cup (3½ ounces/100 grams) turbinado sugar, for coating the cookies

(Chocolate filling ingredients follow on the next page.)

1. Make the cookie dough: Into a medium bowl, sift together the flour, cocoa powder, cinnamon, ginger, allspice, baking soda, and salt.

2. In the bowl of an electric mixer fitted with the paddle attachment, beat together the butter, muscovado sugar, and vanilla extract on medium-high speed for about 4 minutes, or until the mixture is noticeably lighter in color, transforming from a dark, gritty-looking mixture to something fluffier and latte-like in color. Beat in the egg until completely absorbed. Beat in the molasses until well blended.

3. Reduce the mixer speed to low and gradually stir in the dry ingredients. Mix until well blended and even in color. Cover the bowl and refrigerate the dough for about 2 hours.

4. When you're ready to bake, position the racks to the upper and lower thirds of the oven and preheat the oven to 350°F. Line 2 baking sheets with parchment paper or silicone baking mats.

5. To form the cookies, pour the turbinado sugar onto a plate. Using a small ice cream scoop with a capacity of about 1 tablespoon, portion the dough into balls. Roll

CHOCOLATE FILLING

2 ounces (57 grams) bittersweet chocolate (60% to 70% cacao)

2 tablespoons (1 ounce/28 grams) unsalted butter, cut into small pieces

½ teaspoon unsulphured molasses

the dough balls in the turbinado sugar, coating them completely. Place on the prepared baking sheets, evenly spacing them with 1 dozen cookies per sheet. Repeat with the balance of the dough.

6. Bake the cookies until they are set on the edges, but still very soft in the centers, about 10 minutes. Quickly pull the sheets from the oven (close the oven door so as to not let all the heat escape!). Using deft thumbs, a spoon with a very deep well (like a melon baller), or a thick-handled wooden spoon, make a deep indentation in the center of each cookie. Return to the oven to finish baking, about 5 minutes more. Let the cookies cool on the pans set over wire racks. If the indentations have become shallow, press them down again while the cookies are warm.

7. Make the filling: Place the chocolate and butter in a heatproof bowl. Melt in the microwave with 30-second bursts of high heat, stirring well after each interval. Stir in the molasses. Transfer the ganache to a small zip-top bag and work it toward the corner of the bag. Snip off a tiny bit at the corner. Fill each cookie with ganache. Let the cookies set at room temperature until the ganache is firm, about 1 hour.

8. Store the cookies in an airtight container at room temperature for up to 5 days.

Chocolate-Slicked Chewy Crispy Bars

MAKES SIXTEEN 2-INCH SQUARES

These bars are a raw sugar riff on the Scotcharoo, a tooth-achingly sweet treat from my mid-western upbringing. They're also reminiscent of the American Whatchamacallit bars (which I fear are now considered "retro"), and the Special Crisp bar in Canada.

2½ cups (3 ounces/85 grams) crispy rice cereal

⅓ cup (4 ounces/113 grams) brown rice syrup

⅓ cup (2⅝ ounces/75 grams) firmly packed dark muscovado sugar

½ teaspoon fine sea salt

½ cup (4½ ounces/128 grams) natural peanut butter, preferably the crunchy, salt-added variety

½ teaspoon pure vanilla extract

½ cup (3 ounces/85 grams) bittersweet chocolate chips (60% to 70% cacao)

1 teaspoon coconut, grapeseed, or canola oil

1. Line an 8 × 8-inch baking pan with aluminum foil or parchment paper. Spray the pan lightly with nonstick cooking spray.

2. Pour the cereal into a large mixing bowl.

3. In a small saucepan, stir together the brown rice syrup, sugar, and salt. Place the pan over medium heat. Stir gently as the syrup heats. When the sugar is dissolved and the syrup just begins to bubble around the edges, remove the pan from the heat—do not let the syrup boil. Add the peanut butter and vanilla extract, stirring until the peanut butter is completely melted.

4. Pour the goo over the cereal. Stir a few times with a large flexible spatula. Once the syrup has cooled enough to handle, spray a bit of nonstick spray on your hands and use your fingertips to lightly toss the mixture until the cereal is completely coated. Turn the coated cereal into the prepared pan and press it lightly and evenly, being careful not to compact the cereal too firmly, or the bars will come out hard instead of chewy. Let cool at room temperature for about 15 minutes.

5. Meanwhile, put the chocolate chips and oil in a heatproof bowl. Melt together in the microwave with 30-second bursts of high heat, stirring well after each interval until smooth. Pour the chocolate over the bars. Using a pastry brush, "paint" the surface of the bars with the chocolate for a thin, even coating. Refrigerate until the chocolate is set, about 20 minutes, before cutting into bars. Store in an airtight container at room temperature.

TIP: *This recipe doubles easily—just use a medium saucepan for the syrup with the same cooking time, and pat the crispy mixture into a 9 × 13-inch pan instead.*

HOMEMADE INFUSED NATURAL SUGARS

When it comes to big flavors in baked goods, I sometimes like to take the more-is-more approach. Infusing already flavorful natural sugars with an array of ambrosial, herbal, floral, or spicy notes is a really fun way not only to make your favorite recipes really sing but also to impress everyone you know with your mad DIY skills and the ultimate edible gift.

   It couldn't be simpler to shake up a batch of any infused sugar you can dream up. Here's the idea:

2 cups (7 ounces/200 grams) of your favorite dry natural sugar	+	A handful of your favorite herbs, whole spices, or edible dried flowers	+	One 1-pint (16 ounces/453 grams) jar with a tight-fitting lid

= Homemade Infused Natural Sugar

When I set out to make a batch of infused sugar, I think about flavor pairings first. My favorite candidates are evaporated cane juice, because of its rather neutral flavor, and coarse, sparkly turbinado (especially for gifting, with its light caramel vibe and gourmet look). But more intensely flavored dry sugars (such as coconut sugar or rapadura) pair really well with bold spices in an entirely different way.

For flavorings, my favorite choices for herbs are mint, basil, and rosemary; although you can use fresh or dried herbs, fresh is especially nice. To prepare them, gently tear leafy herbs or lightly crush tougher ones, such as rosemary—the idea is to just bruise them a bit to begin to release the fragrant and flavorful essential oils, not to chop them so finely that they become damp and make your sugar clumpy. The same goes for citrus—use finely sliced strips of orange, lemon, lime, or grapefruit peels, pith and all, rather than grate off the zest, which can be very moist.

Dried edible flowers are fabulous for infusing sugars, but remember: a little goes a long way. Just a few rosebuds or sprigs of lavender are plenty for a single jar. Be sure to look for flowers that are unsprayed—tea shops are an excellent source of flowers that are safe for eating and sugar infusing.

Fresh vanilla beans split lengthwise are a given for infused sugars and will create a jar of heavenly sweetness into which you can't resist stuffing your nose. Whole spices like cinnamon sticks, peppercorns, star anise, and cardamom are also wonderful—just lightly crack the sticks, seeds, or pods with a mortar and pestle or the side of a heavy knife to break them up a bit before tucking them into a jar of sugar.

No matter what flavorings you use to infuse, give the jar of sugar a good shake every couple of days, and let the sugar infuse for at least a week before using or gifting. The best thing is that it's quite literally the gift that keeps on giving—as you use the sugar, just pour some fresh sugar back into the jar, give it a good shake, and the flavor party keeps on going. Use infused sugars as you would extracts or oils in baked goods—add a few spoonfuls in batters or doughs; spoon it into coffee or tea; rim a cocktail glass; or scatter some over cookies, scones, or muffins before baking for a fragrant, sweet sparkle.

Maple Sugar Butter Cookies

MAKES ABOUT 3 DOZEN 2-INCH COOKIES

This is a super maple-charged riff on an old family recipe for the sugar cookies that I've loved every Christmas since I can remember. They're buttery, crisp, and a bit sandy in texture. If you invest in a canister of good maple sugar, this is the kind of simple recipe that can really let it shine.

1¼ cups (5⅜ ounces/152 grams) whole wheat pastry flour, spooned and leveled

1¼ cups (5⅝ ounces/160 grams) unbleached all-purpose flour, spooned and leveled

½ teaspoon baking soda

½ teaspoon cream of tartar

½ teaspoon fine sea salt

½ cup (4 ounces/113 grams) grapeseed or canola oil

1 large egg

1 teaspoon pure vanilla extract

½ cup (1 stick/4 ounces/113 grams) unsalted butter, at room temperature

¾ cup (4⅞ ounces/138 grams) pure maple sugar plus some for sprinkling

1. Position the racks in the upper and lower thirds of the oven and preheat the oven to 350°F. Line 2 baking sheets with parchment paper.

2. Into a large bowl, sift together the flours, baking soda, cream of tartar, and salt.

3. In a large measuring cup, whisk together the oil, egg, and vanilla extract until well blended.

4. In the bowl of an electric mixer fitted with the paddle attachment, beat together the butter and maple sugar on medium-high speed until smooth and lighter in texture, about 3 minutes (the sugar granules will still be obvious). Reduce the speed to medium and slowly pour in the oil and egg mixture. Increase the speed to medium-high and beat for 3 minutes, scraping down the bowl often. At the end of the beating time, bits of maple sugar will still be visible, but the overall texture of the mixture will be light, smooth, and glossy, like mayonnaise.

5. Reduce the mixer speed to low and gradually stir in the flour mixture. When just a few traces of flour remain, fold the dough by hand to ensure even mixing (the dough will be very soft).

6. Using a 1-tablespoon-size scoop, portion the dough onto the 2 prepared baking sheets, 1 dozen cookies per sheet. Use the first 3 fingers of your hands to lightly flatten each dough ball to a ¼-inch thickness. Lightly sprinkle each cookie with a pinch of maple sugar. Bake until golden at the edges and underneath (the cookies should be firm enough to lift and check the color). Let the cookies cool on the sheets for 2 minutes before removing to a wire rack to cool completely. Repeat the portioning, flattening, and sprinkling process with the remaining dough.

Picnics and Potlucks

HAVING GROWN UP IN THE MIDWEST, I'm a sucker for comfort foods that serve a crowd, especially desserts. We are a people who believe in hospitality via a 9 × 13-inch baking dish. It's a beautiful thing. When I think of all the reasons that we invest time in home baking, having a solid handful of go-to recipes that can easily travel along to a picnic or potluck is up there with holiday cookies. It's the stuff of community and tradition, the kinds of goodies that draw people to a buffet table and get them talking. And nothing gets people talking quite like learning that a dessert is made without white granulated sugar. These might be my most favorite recipes of all.

Coconut Sugar Banana Sheet Cake with Caramelized Coconut Sugar Frosting

MAKES ONE 9 × 13-INCH CAKE

Although it's not a perfect fit for every baked good, when you find the right recipe to use coconut sugar, it's as though the heavens open up as you take a bite. Because it's not derived from sugarcane, the "brown" flavor of coconut sugar doesn't come from molasses, and so it tastes quite different from other brown sugars like turbinado or muscovado. It's a decidedly exotic, toasty flavor that pairs wonderfully with other tropical flavors, especially bananas.

Speaking of bananas, one of the tricks of using coconut sugar successfully in baking is to find a recipe that has plenty of tenderizing, moisture-lending ingredients in it—such as mashed bananas or other fruit purees, oils, and buttermilk or yogurt—as coconut sugar tends to dry out baked goods.

2 cups (9 ounces/255 grams) unbleached all-purpose flour,* spooned and leveled

2 teaspoons baking powder

½ teaspoon baking soda

½ teaspoon fine sea salt

1⅓ cups (10⅝ ounces/302 grams) mashed bananas (from about 3 very ripe medium ones)

⅔ cup (5⅓ ounces/151 grams) 2% Greek yogurt

¼ cup (2 ounces/57 grams) coconut or canola oil

1 cup plus 2 tablespoons (6 ounces/170 grams) coconut sugar

1. Position a rack in the center of the oven and preheat the oven to 350°F. Spray a 9 × 13-inch pan with nonstick spray or butter it generously.

2. Into a medium bowl, sift together the flour, baking powder, baking soda, and salt.

3. In a separate medium bowl, whisk together the bananas, yogurt, and oil until smooth.

4. In the bowl of an electric mixer fitted with the paddle attachment, beat together the sugar and butter on medium-low speed until the mixture looks like dampened sand, about 1 minute. Add the eggs one at a

*A mix of half all-purpose, half whole wheat pastry flour works well here, too.

4 tablespoons (2 ounces/57 grams) unsalted butter, at room temperature

2 large eggs, at room temperature

1 teaspoon pure vanilla extract

1 batch Caramelized Coconut Sugar Frosting (see page 227)

time, giving the first about 30 seconds to incorporate before adding the second. Increase the speed to medium-high, beating until light in texture and much paler in color, 4 to 5 minutes (don't skimp on the beating time here—the significant change in color will be your cue that the sugar has begun to dissolve). Beat in the vanilla extract.

5. Reduce the mixer speed to low. Stir in the dry ingredients and banana-yogurt mixture in five alternating additions, beginning and ending with the dry ingredients, letting each addition fully absorb into the batter before adding the next. Finish folding the batter gently by hand to ensure it is well blended.

6. Scrape the batter into the prepared pan and smooth the top. Bake until a toothpick comes out clean, 25 to 30 minutes. Cool the cake completely in the pan on a wire rack. Keeping the cake in the pan for easy transport and storage, slather with the frosting.

Must I Sift?

Ah, a question for the ages. I hear this question often from home bakers who are wondering if it's really necessary to sift together dry ingredients with a sieve or other sifting tool, as opposed to just whisking or stirring the flours, leaveners, powders, and so on in a recipe.

So is sifting essential? For me, the answer is sometimes. Much of it depends on the ingredients you're working with, the conditions in your own individual kitchen, and the recipe you're making.

In San Francisco where I live and bake, the air can get quite humid, and I find that dry ingredients like flours, cocoa powder, spices, confectioners' sugar, baking powder, and baking soda tend to clump up during shipping and storage more so than in drier climates. It only takes one soapy bite of a lump of baking soda in an otherwise perfect slice of cake to convince you that maybe that sifting step might have been a good choice.

There's also the issue of how flour is measured in a recipe if you're measuring by volume, using cups and spoons. The recipes in this book use the "spooned and leveled" method of flour measuring (see page 18), and the flour doesn't have to be sifted first. In other books, however, you might see that flour is listed as "1 cup sifted flour," and in that case you must sift the flour first, deposit it into the cup, and level the top. This makes for a much lighter cup of flour, which affects the outcome of the whole recipe. If you're measuring by weight, however, this isn't an issue, and sifting is only a function of aerating the flour and making sure there are no gritty bits in the mix.

Another thing to keep in mind is the texture of the finished baked goods. Generally, I find that the lighter the texture of the finished baked goods, the more apt I am to sift the dry ingredients together rather than just whisk. If it's just flour and I'm making a pretty sturdy item like a cookie or quick bread, I'll often whisk the flour to aerate it and while doing so give a good look for any pesky clumps. But if it's a lighter cake, I'll always sift the drys.

Working in the natural-sugars kitchen, though, I lean toward sifting in general—the less processed an ingredient is, the more coarse the texture can be, and a little extra de-clumping insurance, plus some aeration, is never a bad thing.

Banana Butterscotch Cream Pie

MAKES ONE 9-INCH PIE

If ever there was a "project pie," this is it. But I promise you that every minute of your time will be worth it. To relieve the pressure of making all the elements in one fell swoop, know that the building blocks of this creamy, sweet-salty masterpiece can be made a day ahead. All you need to do is make sure the pastry cream and butterscotch sauce are allowed to warm up a bit out of the fridge and then whisked until smooth before putting everything together and giving the assembled pie a final chill.

BROWN SUGAR PASTRY CREAM

2 cups (16 ounces/454 grams) whole milk

½ vanilla bean, split lengthwise

4 large egg yolks

1 whole large egg

6 tablespoons (3 ounces/85 grams) firmly packed light muscovado sugar

¼ teaspoon fine sea salt

4 tablespoons (1⅛ ounces/32 grams) cornstarch

2 tablespoons (1 ounce/28 grams) unsalted butter, cut into small pieces

1 teaspoon pure vanilla extract

BUTTERSCOTCH SAUCE

4 tablespoons (2 ounces/57 grams) unsalted butter, cut into small pieces

½ cup (4 ounces/113 grams) firmly packed light muscovado sugar

¼ cup (2⅛ ounces/60 grams) heavy cream

¼ teaspoon fine sea salt

½ teaspoon pure vanilla extract

ASSEMBLY AND TOPPING

1 Whole Wheat All-Butter Pie Crust (see page 245), blind-baked (see page 244) and cooled

3 medium firm-ripe bananas

1¼ cups (10⅝ ounces/301 grams) heavy cream, chilled

1 tablespoon organic confectioners' sugar

½ teaspoon pure vanilla extract

TIP: *Accidentally overcooking stovetop custards happens to the best of us. If your pastry cream is looking a bit lumpy in the saucepan, don't fret—it will smooth out perfectly with a quick blitz in a blender.*

TIP: *Although it's best to serve the pie soon after its final chill, the pie can be assembled and refrigerated up to 1 day ahead.*

1. Make the pastry cream: In a large saucepan set over medium heat, combine the milk and vanilla bean. Bring it to a bare simmer, but don't let it boil. Remove the pan from the heat. Cover the pot and steep for 10 minutes. Pull out the vanilla pod, and using the back of a small knife, scrape any remaining vanilla seeds into the milk. Discard the pod.

2. In a large bowl, energetically whisk together the egg yolks, egg, muscovado sugar, and salt until noticeably paler in color, about 1 minute. Whisk in the cornstarch. Slowly whisk in the hot milk until well blended. Pour the mixture back into the saucepan. Set the pan over low heat and stir constantly with a flexible heatproof spatula, gently scraping any clinging custard from the bottom and sides of the pan until the pastry cream is very thick and just beginning to bubble, about 5 minutes.

3. Pour the custard into a blender. Add the butter and vanilla extract and blend on high speed for 1 minute. Transfer the custard to a clean bowl and cover the surface with a sheet of plastic wrap to prevent a skin from forming. Chill in the refrigerator for at least 2 hours, or up to 1 day ahead.

4. Make the butterscotch sauce: In a medium heavy-bottomed saucepan over medium heat, melt the butter. Whisk in the muscovado sugar until dissolved. Slowly pour in the cream and salt, whisking to blend. Bring the sauce to a boil and then immediately reduce the heat to low—you want the sauce to be gently bubbling away, not at a violent boil. Cook for 3 minutes, stirring often. Remove the pan from the heat. Stir in the vanilla extract. Pour into a heatproof bowl and cover the bowl with plastic wrap. Chill in the refrigerator for at least 1 hour or up to 2 days before assembling the pie.

5. Now the moment of truth—assembling this glorious pie! Set the prepared pie shell in the refrigerator to chill for 30 minutes. Meanwhile, remove the pastry cream and butterscotch sauce from the fridge and allow them to warm up a bit at room temperature for about 30 minutes. Separately, whisk the pastry cream and butterscotch sauce until smooth.

6. Pour the pastry cream into the chilled shell and smooth the top. Slice the bananas on the diagonal into ½-inch-thick slices, and arrange them over the pastry cream. Spread the butterscotch sauce over the bananas.

7. In a medium bowl with a handheld electric mixer, whip the cream to stiff peaks with the confectioners' sugar and vanilla extract. Top the pie with the whipped cream. Chill the assembled pie for at least 1 hour before slicing and serving.

Maple Chocolate Cake

MAKES TWO 9-INCH CAKE LAYERS, ONE 9 × 13-INCH SHEET CAKE, OR ABOUT 1½ DOZEN CUPCAKES

The one-bowl chocolate cake is a busy baker's workhorse, and a concept that's been riffed on in countless ways by just about every cookbook, food magazine, and professional domestic goddess over the past few decades. And for good reason—who doesn't love being minutes away from homemade chocolate cake, no complicated machinery required? My version is naturally sweetened with maple syrup, which also makes it unbeatably moist.

1½ cups (6¾ ounces/192 grams) unbleached all-purpose flour, spooned and leveled

¾ cup (2½ ounces/72 grams) unsweetened natural cocoa powder

1½ teaspoons baking soda

¾ teaspoon baking powder

¾ teaspoon fine sea salt

1 cup (11⅞ ounces/336 grams) pure maple syrup (dark or very dark preferred)✱

1 cup (8½ ounces/242 grams) 2% Greek yogurt

2 large eggs

¼ cup (2 ounces/57 grams) grapeseed or canola oil

1 teaspoon pure vanilla extract

✱ I like honey here, too. It creates a noticeably different flavor profile when combined with cocoa, which makes this recipe great for mixing and matching with a variety of frostings and toppings.

1. Position racks in the upper and lower thirds of the oven and preheat the oven to 350°F.

2. Lightly grease a 9 × 13-inch rectangular baking pan or two 9-inch round pans (and line them with parchment paper), or line 18 wells of two 12-cup muffin tins with paper liners.

3. Into a large bowl, sift together the flour, cocoa powder, baking soda, baking powder, and salt.

4. In a large measuring cup or medium bowl, whisk together the maple syrup, yogurt, eggs, oil, and vanilla extract.

5. Pour the wet ingredients into the dry. Using a whisk, energetically blend the batter by hand until smooth and thick, about 1 minute. Spread the batter into the prepared pan or pans. (For cupcakes, fill the cups no more than two-thirds full—you should get 18 cupcakes.)

6. Bake until a toothpick inserted into the center comes out clean and the tops of the cakes spring back when lightly touched, 30 to 35 minutes for sheet and layer cakes, or 20 minutes for cupcakes. Cool completely in the pan or pans on a wire rack before inverting and frosting.

Cinnamon-Sugared Blueberry Bundt
(opposite)

Chocolate Chip and Cherry Date Cake
(page 106)

Cinnamon-Sugared Blueberry Bundt

MAKES ONE 10-INCH BUNDT CAKE

Like peacefully sleeping babies, baskets of puppies, and stacks of cold, hard cash, there's just something undeniably appealing about an enormous Bundt cake. Especially one with the sparkle and crunch of turbinado sugar. A swirl of cinnamon and a smattering of tiny blueberries that pop like fruity caviar seal the deal in this crowd-pleaser.

PREPARING THE PAN

¼ cup (1¾ ounces/50 grams) turbinado sugar

¾ teaspoon ground cinnamon*

CAKE

1½ cups (6¾ ounces/192 grams) unbleached all-purpose flour, spooned and leveled, plus 1 extra teaspoon for dusting the berries

1½ cups (6⅜ ounces/181 grams) whole wheat pastry flour, spooned and leveled

2½ teaspoons baking powder

½ teaspoon baking soda

1 teaspoon fine sea salt

1½ cups (10½ ounces/300 grams) turbinado sugar

1¼ cups (2½ sticks/10 ounces/283 grams) unsalted butter, at room temperature

2 teaspoons pure vanilla extract

4 large eggs, at room temperature

1½ cups (12¾ ounces/362 grams) well-shaken buttermilk, at room temperature

1½ cups (7½ ounces/210 grams) frozen organic wild blueberries**

1. Position a rack in the lower third of the oven and preheat the oven to 350°F.

2. Prepare the pan: Spray a 10-inch Bundt pan with nonstick cooking spray, hitting all the little dips and creases in the pan with spray.

3. In a small bowl, stir together the sugar and cinnamon. Sprinkle the cinnamon sugar all over the inside of the pan, turning it to coat as much surface area of the pan as possible.

4. Make the cake: In a medium bowl, whisk together the flours, baking powder, baking soda, and salt. Set aside.

5. In the bowl of an electric mixer fitted with the paddle attachment, beat together the sugar and butter on medium-high speed until lightened in color and fluffy, about 5 minutes total. About 1 minute into the beating

* I just can't get enough of the spicy, bold sweetness of Vietnamese cinnamon. Look for it in specialty stores or in stores that sell fresh spices in bulk.

** Keep the blueberries in the freezer right up until the time you toss them with flour and fold them into the batter. This will keep the berries from bursting as you mix and staining the batter with a greenish cast.

time, add the vanilla extract. Beat in the eggs one at a time, letting each one blend into the batter for about 30 seconds before adding the next.

6. Reduce the mixer speed to low and add about half the flour, mixing just until the flour begins to disappear. Add the buttermilk, mixing to incorporate. Add the rest of the flour and mix until there are a few streaks of flour left in the batter. Fold by hand several times with a large spatula until the batter is smooth.

7. Remove the blueberries from the freezer and divide in half. Place half the berries in a small bowl and toss with 1 teaspoon of all-purpose flour. Quickly and gently fold the floured berries into the batter and spread the batter into the prepared pan. Sprinkle the rest of the berries on top of the batter. Bake until a toothpick inserted in the center comes out clean, about 1 hour. Cool completely in the pan on a wire rack. Invert the cake onto a serving platter. Store any leftovers in an airtight container or cake dome at room temperature for up to 3 days.

Turbinado: the hero

Weight: 1 cup/7 ounces/200 grams

Characteristics: Rough around the edges but can save the day with its versatility, coarse, crunchy, light molasses flavor, rounded sweetness. Also known as demerara sugar.

Where it comes from: Turbinado sugar comes from sugarcane and is produced around the globe. It's the "raw sugar" that's the result of the centrifuge-spinning stage in the sugar production process (see page 16 for more on that operation). That centrifuge can also be a called a turbine, hence the term "turbinado" sugar. Depending on the producer, the depth of molasses flavor and the color of turbinado sugar can vary.

Demerara sugar is essentially the same thing as turbinado, and you'll often find the terms used interchangeably ("demerara" is the term of choice in Britain, for example). Typically, sugar that is labeled as demerara tends to be a touch lighter in color with a blondish hue and slightly less intense in flavor than turbinado. Both turbinado and demerara sugars are also sometimes referred to as "raw sugar" in recipes and cookbooks.

Best uses: Although it's much coarser and sometimes doesn't yield as fine a texture, turbinado sugar usually makes for a reasonable 1:1 swap for white granulated sugar. (Sometimes I love the nubbly texture that turbinado gives baked goods, such as Mrs. Braun's Oatmeal Cookies on page 68.) When in doubt, it helps to grind turbinado finer in a food processor, or use it in recipes where it can be allowed to completely dissolve, like a sugar syrup for candy, or meringues using the Swiss method (see "A Tale of Two Meringues" on page 185), or simply given extra time to break down with additional beating time (always in the earlier stages of a recipe, before the flour is added).

But what turbinado lacks in delicacy, it more than makes up for it with flavor and crunch. There's nothing like a streusel topping made with this hearty, sparkling sugar, and it's ideal for sprinkling over cookies, cakes, muffins, and scones before baking for a pretty but decidedly natural and rustic look.

Bonus points: Turbinado sugar is less processed than white granulated sugar and not treated with chemicals. Although it's not a superstar in terms of nutritional value, turbinado hasn't been stripped of all its molasses and therefore does contain traces of calcium, iron, potassium, magnesium, phosphorus, and some B vitamins.

How to store: The bit of molasses that still remains in turbinado can tend to keep some brands from staying dry and free-flowing. A cool, dry storage place and a tightly sealed container are your best bets to keep turbinado from absorbing more moisture from the air.

Chocolate Chip and Cherry Date Cake

MAKES ONE 8-INCH CAKE

Oh, how I adore this cake. Perfect for everything from countertop snacking to a holiday buffet, it's an insanely flavorful, moist, and naturally sweetened phenom. Except for a handful of dark muscovado for stickiness and depth, the majority of the sweetness here comes from dates, a magical little superfood that's a boon when baking with natural sugars.

Here, the dates are soaked and then pull double duty—some of them are soaked longer, and pureed into a paste to sweeten and moisten the cake (you can learn more about this awesome white sugar alternative on page 55). The rest of the chopped dates get a shorter bath, and are used for texture in the cake, along with dried sweet cherries and little nubs of bittersweet chocolate. The tiniest hit of orange zest dials up the fruity sweetness of the dates, so don't skip it.

This recipe is pictured on page 102.

12 ounces (340 grams) pitted Deglet Noor dates, coarsely chopped*

⅓ cup (1¾ ounces/50 grams) dried cherries

1½ cups (6¾ ounces/192 grams) unbleached all-purpose flour, spooned and leveled

1 teaspoon baking soda

¾ teaspoon fine sea salt

½ cup (4 ounces/113 grams) firmly packed dark muscovado sugar

2 large eggs

1 teaspoon finely grated orange zest

1 teaspoon pure vanilla extract

12 tablespoons (1½ sticks/6 ounces/170 grams) unsalted butter, melted and cooled

⅓ cup (2 ounces/57 grams) bittersweet chocolate (60% to 70% cacao), chopped

1. Position a rack in the center of the oven and preheat the oven to 350°F. Lightly grease an 8-inch round cake pan and line it with a circle of parchment paper.

2. Start by prepping the dates, dividing them between 2 small heatproof bowls: Place 7 ounces (about 1 cup) into one bowl and add the cherries. Place the remaining 5 ounces (about ¾ cup) into the other bowl. Cover the fruit in both bowls with boiling water. Set aside to soften—you'll need to soak the dates with the cherries for just 10 minutes, while the rest of the dates require a 20-minute soak.

*The two date varieties you're most likely to find are Deglet Noor and Medjool. The commercial, packaged dates that you'll find whole or chopped in most supermarkets are usually Deglet Noor. They're firmer and drier than Medjool dates, so they're easier to chop into bits for baking, and are a more economical choice when you need a lot for a single recipe, like this cake.

3. In a large bowl, whisk together the flour, baking soda, and salt.

4. After 10 minutes of soaking time, drain the bowl containing the dates and cherries, and pat the fruit dry with paper towels. Set aside.

5. Ten minutes later, drain the other bowl of dates, reserving the liquid. Place these dates in the bowl of a food processor fitted with the steel blade. Puree into a paste, adding a teaspoon or two of the soaking liquid as needed, stopping often to scrape down the bowl. When the paste is smooth, you should have about 1 cup paste (see page 55 for more details on date paste). To the food processor, add the sugar, eggs, orange zest, and vanilla. Process until lightened in color, aerated, and smooth, about 1 minute. With the processor running, pour the melted butter into the feed tube and process for 1 minute more. Pour the wet ingredients into the bowl with the flour mixture. Use a flexible spatula to fold the batter until well blended. Fold in the soaked dates and cherries and then fold in the chocolate bits.

6. Scrape the batter into the prepared pan and bake until a toothpick inserted into the center comes out clean, 50 to 55 minutes. Let the cake cool in the pan on a wire rack before inverting onto a serving platter.

TIP: *This simple cake can go from coffee break snack to dessert superstar with a dollop of flavored whipped cream (think citrus zest, a sprinkle of warming spices like cinnamon, or a combination of both).*

Spiced, Brûléed Maple Pumpkin Pie

SERVES 10 TO 12

I'm all about adding a little twist on the traditional, and this crème brûlée meets pumpkin pie fits the bill perfectly. Whipped cream is truly optional when your pumpkin pie is jazzed up like this one.

¾ cup plus 2 tablespoons (7½ ounces/212 grams) heavy cream

1½ teaspoons ground cinnamon

¾ teaspoon ground ginger

2 star anise

2 large eggs

2 large egg yolks

⅔ cup (4⅜ ounces/123 grams) pure maple sugar

2 tablespoons (½ ounce/16 grams) cornstarch

¼ teaspoon fine sea salt

1¾ cups (1 15-ounce can/425 grams) solid-pack pumpkin puree

2 teaspoons pure vanilla extract

1 Whole Wheat All-Butter Pie Crust (see page 245), blind-baked (see page 244) and cooled

¼ cup (1¾ ounces/50 grams) turbinado sugar, for topping

1. Position a rack in the center of the oven and preheat the oven to 325°F.

2. In a small saucepan, heat the cream just until it begins to simmer. Whisk in the cinnamon and ginger, and toss in the star anise. Cover the pot and let steep for 10 minutes.

3. In a large bowl, combine the eggs, egg yolks, maple sugar, cornstarch, and salt. Whisk energetically for at least 2 minutes, or until the mixture is thickened and lightened in color.

4. Remove the star anise from the saucepan. Whisk the cream into the egg mixture. Whisk in the pumpkin and vanilla extract until the filling is smooth.

5. Pour the filling into the pie shell. Bake until the filling is just set around the outer third of the pie, and wobbly toward the center, 50 to 55 minutes. If the crust begins to darken too quickly, protect it with a collar crafted from aluminum foil. Turn off the oven, and let the pie cool in the oven with the door cracked for 10 minutes. Remove and let cool completely on a wire rack. Refrigerate for 2 hours.

6. Right before you're about to serve the pie, it's time to turn this baby into a brûléed masterpiece. Sprinkle the surface of the pie with an even layer of turbinado sugar.

Use a kitchen torch to caramelize the sugar until it's deeply browned and bubbling. Alternatively, if your pie is in a ceramic plate or tin that can withstand a broiler (many glass plates cannot—check the bottom of the plate for any warnings), you can protect the crust with foil, and broil the sugar with high heat for about 1 minute, keeping a close watch on it as the sugar caramelizes.

Orange-Scented Vanilla Bean and Turbinado Pound Cake

MAKES ONE 9 × 5-INCH LOAF CAKE

When you're making a recipe that uses the creaming method (wherein butter and sugar are beaten together at the beginning of the recipe), one of the functions of sugar is to punch lots of tiny holes in the butter to create little pockets that can then fill up and expand with hot air and create a nice rise during baking. Granulated white sugar works great for creaming because it's so fine; when you're baking with coarser natural sugars, getting fine-textured cakes with the creaming method can be a toughie.

One of the tricks to making coarse turbinado sugar work in place of granulated sugar is extra mixing time anywhere you can fit it in, before the flour is added. Additional beating helps the turbinado break down a bit and aerate the butter and eggs. So be sure to pay attention to the beating times here—3 to 4 minutes for creaming the butter and sugar, then 1 whole minute after each egg is added. It seems pushy of me to inflict all this extra beating time on you, but the airy, cloudlike batter makes it all worth it.

¾ cup (3¼ ounces/90 grams) whole wheat pastry flour, spooned and leveled

¾ cup (3⅜ ounces/96 grams) unbleached all-purpose flour, spooned and leveled

½ teaspoon fine sea salt

¼ teaspoon baking soda

1¼ cups (8¾ ounces/250 grams) turbinado sugar, plus extra for sprinkling

2 teaspoons finely grated orange zest

½ cup (1 stick/4 ounces/113 grams) unsalted butter, at room temperature

1 tablespoon vanilla bean paste* or pure vanilla extract

¼ teaspoon pure almond extract

3 large eggs, at room temperature

¼ cup (2 ounces/57 grams) freshly squeezed orange juice

¼ cup (2⅛ ounces/60 grams) 2% Greek yogurt

*Vanilla bean paste is one of my favorite baking ingredients—it has huge vanilla flavor, plus the aesthetic beauty of all those flecks, without having to scrape a bean.

1. Position a rack in the lower third of the oven and preheat the oven to 350°F. Butter a 9 × 5-inch loaf pan and line with parchment paper.

2. Into a medium bowl, sift together the flours, salt, and baking soda.

3. In a small bowl, combine the sugar and orange zest. Using your fingertips, massage the zest into the sugar until it is fragrant and moist.

4. In the bowl of an electric mixer fitted with the paddle attachment, combine the butter, orange-scented sugar, vanilla bean paste, and almond extract. Beat on medium-high speed until light and fluffy, 3 to 4 minutes. With the mixer running, beat in the eggs one at a time, allowing 1 minute of mixing time after each addition.

5. In a small bowl, whisk together the orange juice and yogurt until smooth.

6. Reduce the mixer speed to low. Slowly add the dry ingredients. When no dry pockets remain, stir in the orange juice and yogurt mixture. Give the batter a quick folding by hand to ensure everything is incorporated. Scrape the batter into the prepared pan and smooth the top. Sprinkle the top generously with sugar.

7. Bake until a toothpick inserted deeply into the very center comes out clean, about 1 hour.

8. Cool completely in the pan on a wire rack before slicing.

TIP: *Here's a life tip. You know how whole wheat flour—even finely milled whole wheat pastry flour—can sometimes add a faintly bitter taste to baked goods? Adding a couple tablespoons of orange juice to the batter in place of some of the liquid in a recipe (like water or milk) neutralizes that tannic flavor. Really! Here the orange juice is a major flavor player because it's paired with zest, but in other recipes you can't really detect the citrus notes. Give it a shot!*

Rummy Roasted Pineapple Pudding Cake

MAKES ONE 8 × 8-INCH CAKE

From the outset, this appears to be any streusel-topped, brown-sugary crumb cake. But tucked within is a gold mine of caramelized, roasted pineapple chunks. And below that? Well, would you believe me when I tell you that this cake actually makes its own *sauce*? True story.

Now, to be fair, this cake requires a few steps, but I promise you the effort is worth it. And even though you will reach a point where you think to yourself, *Am I really pouring hot liquid over a cake batter? Is this* cooking *the batter on contact? This broad's lost it!* I hope you'll trust me. This cake with a scoop of vanilla ice cream is dessert dynamite. *Boom.*

ROASTED PINEAPPLE

1½ cups (10½ ounces/296 grams) pineapple, fresh or canned and drained (juice reserved), cut into 1-inch chunks*****

1 tablespoon (½ ounce/14 grams) firmly packed dark muscovado sugar

STREUSEL

¼ cup (1⅛ ounces/32 grams) unbleached all-purpose flour, spooned and leveled

3 tablespoons (1½ ounces/42 grams) firmly packed dark muscovado sugar

2 tablespoons (1 ounce/28 grams) unsalted butter, chilled and cut into small pieces

1 tablespoon turbinado sugar (optional)******

Pinch of fine sea salt

(Cake and sauce ingredients follow on the next page.)

1. Position a rack in the center of the oven and preheat the oven to 450°F. Line a rimmed baking sheet with parchment paper.

2. Prepare the pineapple: Toss the pineapple chunks on the baking sheet with the muscovado sugar until the fruit bits are evenly coated with an amber glaze. Roast, rotating the pan once, until the pineapple chunks are tender and caramelized at the edges, 15 to 20 minutes. Remove the pan from the oven and let the pineapple cool on the sheet pan as you move on to the rest of the recipe.

* You can cut up fresh fruit and buy the juice separately if you're the ambitious type. Or you can get yourself a 20-ounce can of good-quality pineapple chunks packed in 100% fruit juice—they're exactly the right size for this recipe, and when you drain off the juice, you should end up with 1 cup of pineapple juice for the sauce.

** This simply adds sparkle and crunch to the topping. If you have turbinado on hand, add it. If not, the streusel will be perfectly fine without.

CAKE

1 cup (4½ ounces/128 grams) unbleached all-purpose flour, spooned and leveled

2 teaspoons baking powder

¼ teaspoon baking soda

¼ teaspoon ground cinnamon

¼ teaspoon ground ginger

¼ teaspoon fine sea salt

¾ cup (6 ounces/170 grams) firmly packed dark muscovado sugar

⅓ cup (2⅝ ounces/75 grams) whole milk

1 large egg

2 tablespoons (1 ounce/28 grams) canola or grapeseed oil

1 teaspoon pure vanilla extract

SAUCE

1 cup (8 ounces/227 grams) pineapple juice

¼ cup (2 ounces/57 grams) firmly packed dark muscovado sugar

2 tablespoons (1 ounce/28 grams) dark rum (such as Myers's)

¼ teaspoon ground cinnamon

3. Lower the oven temperature to 350°F. Grease an 8 × 8-inch square glass baking dish with butter or nonstick spray.

4. Make the streusel: In a small bowl, work together the flour, muscovado sugar, butter, turbinado sugar (if using), and salt until crumbly. Refrigerate.

5. Make the cake: In a large bowl, whisk together the flour, baking powder, baking soda, cinnamon, ginger, and salt.

6. In a medium bowl, whisk together the muscovado sugar, milk, egg, oil, and vanilla extract. Pour the wet ingredients into the flour mixture and whisk until the batter is smooth. Scrape the batter into the prepared pan and smooth the top. Scatter the roasted pineapple chunks evenly over the batter.

7. Make the sauce: Into a medium saucepan, pour the pineapple juice, muscovado sugar, rum, and cinnamon. Place the pan over high heat and whisk to combine. Bring the mixture to a boil, and lower the heat to medium. Boil for 2 minutes. Remove the pan from the heat and carefully pour the hot liquid over the cake batter. Ask no questions—it will look crazy. Carefully transfer the pan to the oven. Bake for 35 to 40 minutes, or until the cake is puffed and the top is mostly set but still appears a bit wobbly and underdone.

8. Holding your fingertips just an inch or two over the pan, gently sprinkle the streusel evenly over the top of the cake—too much streusel dropped from too great a height will deflate the cake. Return the pan to the oven. Bake until a toothpick inserted into the center comes out with a few moist crumbs, about 10 minutes more. Let the cake cool on a wire rack. Serve warm with vanilla ice cream.

Jazzing Up Treats with Natural Food Colorings

Nothing is more evocative of a carefree, non-calorie-counting childhood than swirls of multicolored frosting, piled high on a cupcake. Or a big old hunk of red velvet cake with a gleaming ruby interior. Or homemade lollipops in every color of the rainbow. But with age and wisdom comes the knowledge that, sadly, calories do count, and all that Day-Glo food probably isn't so good for our insides. Happily, there are some awesome natural alternatives for those moments when life calls for vibrantly hued treats (such as on the All-Purpose Cupcakes on page 116).

If you're feeling particularly domestic, there are plenty of online tutorials that can lead you down the path of making your own colorings out of everything from beets to spinach to various spices. DIY divas of the world, I salute you. But for me, I have come across some beautiful, brilliant ready-made natural food colorings from companies like Chef-Master, which make every color you could possibly want with nothing artificial in the mix. They use everything from red cabbage juice to beta-carotene and chlorophyll to create vibrant, flavorless, and all-natural food colorings. Here are a few tips for using natural colorings.

Get ready to treasure hunt. Good ready-made natural food colorings can be hard to find, but the adventure is worth it. Shop online for the best prices for natural food colorings, or ask your closest baking supply store if it can order them for you.

Timing is everything. Natural food colorings have a short shelf life, and oxidation rates depend on the brand and color, so buy a size that you will likely use in a reasonable amount of time.

Go slow. Because the colors are derived from all kinds of ingredients, the viscosity and intensity of different colors can vary. Some are quite thin and liquidy and can change the consistency of whatever you're trying to color, while others are almost gel-like and can thicken things. Add a few drops at a time to get a sense of how quickly the coloring will come out of the bottle and what color intensity it offers.

All-Purpose Cupcakes

MAKES 1 DOZEN CUPCAKES

Tucked within my hoarder-esque stash of cookbooks, I have a *Sunset* magazine recipe collection from 1949. In it are some recipes that really should probably stay in that era (Halibut Loaf De-Luxe, anyone?). But there also are some real gems, including a recipe called Eggless, Milkless, Butterless Cake. With a few tweaks to improve the texture, a cake likely designed to be economical becomes a great recipe for any baker's arsenal, especially considering the wide variety of special diets that people follow these days.

You have many mix-and-match options when it comes to the sweeteners and nondairy milks here. My favorite pairing is full-fat coconut milk for richness plus honey, or agave if I need to make a truly vegan cake. But any combination of the sweeteners, milks, and oils listed below work just fine. This is a great basic cake that can be flavored with a variety of zests, spices, and extracts.

2 cups (9 ounces/255 grams) unbleached all-purpose flour, spooned and leveled

1 teaspoon baking powder

½ teaspoon baking soda

½ teaspoon fine sea salt

1 cup (8 ounces/227 grams) full-fat coconut, soy, or almond milk

¾ cup (8⅞ ounces/252 grams) honey, pure maple syrup, or agave nectar

⅓ cup (2⅝ ounces/75 grams) grapeseed, vegetable, or coconut oil

1 tablespoon freshly squeezed lemon juice

1 tablespoon pure vanilla extract

1. Position a rack in the center of the oven and preheat the oven to 350°F. Line a 12-cup muffin tin with paper liners.

2. In a large bowl, whisk together the flour, baking powder, baking soda, and salt.

3. In a medium bowl, whisk together the milk, honey, oil, lemon juice, and vanilla extract. Pour the wet ingredients into the dry. Beat with a handheld electric mixer on medium-high speed until smooth and slightly aerated, about 2 minutes.

4. Divide the batter among the wells of the muffin tin, filling them about three-quarters full. Bake until lightly golden, a toothpick inserted into the center of the cupcakes comes out clean, and the tops spring back when lightly touched, 18 to 20 minutes. Rotate the pan 180 degrees halfway through the baking time. Let the cakes cool in the pan set on a wire rack for 3 minutes before removing them from the pan to cool completely.

TIP: *The cupcakes pictured here are frosted with My Favorite Vanilla Bean Buttercream (page 235), which can also be veganized by using vegan buttery sticks (such as Earth Balance).*

Moravian Sugar Cake

MAKES ONE 8-INCH ROUND OR SQUARE CAKE

With a yeast-risen, mashed-potato-fortified dough that looks like bread but comes together like a cake, this recipe is wacky, weird, wonderful, and pure comfort food. It's also full of huge muscovado flavor, with little buttery tunnels of spicy, citrus-scented brown sugar sunken into the dimpled surface. The coffee cake of dreams, I'm telling you.

Use a handheld electric mixer to mash the potato right in the pan, and then again for the dough.

CAKE

1 small to medium russet potato, peeled and cut into ½-inch pieces*

1½ cups (6¾ ounces/192 grams) unbleached all-purpose flour, spooned and leveled

2¼ teaspoons (1 packet/¼ ounce/7 grams) instant yeast

½ teaspoon ground cinnamon

¼ teaspoon freshly grated nutmeg

¼ teaspoon fine sea salt

3 tablespoons (1½ ounces/43 grams) unsalted butter, at room temperature

3 tablespoons (1⅜ ounces/38 grams) evaporated cane juice

1½ teaspoons finely grated orange zest

1 large egg, at room temperature

1 teaspoon pure vanilla extract

* You'll have more mashed potato than you need for the dough; I add a little butter and salt to the remainder and call it a baker's treat. Having both the potato and potato liquid warm when they go into the dough will help the yeast do its thing.

1. Lightly grease an 8-inch round or square metal cake pan with butter or nonstick cooking spray.

2. Make the cake: Place the potato chunks in a small saucepan and add enough water to cover them by 2 inches. Place the pan over medium-high heat and boil until the potato is almost falling apart when pierced with the tip of a knife, about 10 minutes. Reserve ¼ cup (2 ounces/57 grams) of the cooking water. Drain the potato. Dump the potato back into the still-hot pot and shake the pan to dry the potato a bit.

3. Using a handheld electric mixer, mash the potato until smooth (you can press the potato through a ricer or a sieve after mashing it to be sure there are no lumps). Measure out ½ cup (3¾ ounces/106 grams) of mashed potato into a small bowl. Add the reserved cooking water to the bowl. Whisk until smooth.

4. In a medium bowl, whisk together the flour, yeast, cinnamon, nutmeg, and salt.

5. In a large bowl, combine the butter, evaporated cane juice, and orange zest. With the handheld mixer, beat the mixture on medium speed until creamy, about 2 minutes.

SUGAR TOPPING

6 tablespoons (3 ounces/84 grams) firmly packed light or dark muscovado sugar

1 teaspoon ground cinnamon

1½ teaspoons finely grated orange zest

Pinch of fine sea salt

1½ tablespoons (¾ ounce/21 grams) unsalted butter, melted and cooled

Add the egg and beat until smooth and aerated, about 1 minute more. Beat in the vanilla extract. Reduce the mixer speed to low. Add the flour mixture and the potato liquid in 5 alternating additions, beginning and ending with the flour.

6. When the dough is smooth, lightly dust a work surface with all-purpose flour. Scrape out the dough onto the work surface. Flour your hands and knead the dough several times—it will still look a bit shaggy. Drop the dough into the prepared pan and press it into an even layer. Cover the pan with plastic wrap. Allow the dough to rise until doubled in volume, about 1 hour.

7. When you're ready to bake, preheat the oven to 350°F.

8. Make the topping: In a small bowl, fork together the sugar, cinnamon, orange zest, and salt. Dip your index fingers in all-purpose flour and poke 12 to 15 holes all over the surface of the dough, about 1½ inches apart, burrowing all the way to the bottom of the pan. Swirl the tips of your fingers around once they're in the dough, to encourage the holes to stretch a bit and stay open. Fill each hole with a few pinches of the sugar mixture (don't pack it in; just drop it in lightly). Scatter the remaining sugar topping over the surface of the dough. Use a pastry brush to lightly dab and drizzle the melted butter evenly over the surface of the cake.

9. Bake the cake until it is puffed and golden, with a fragrance that fills the kitchen, about 30 minutes. Let cool on a wire rack before inverting the cake onto a platter and serving.

Four-Spice Pear, Apple, and Blackberry Crisp

SERVES 10 TO 12

There is a category of people in this world who endlessly fascinate me: those who forgo cookies, cakes, and ice creams in favor of "just fruit" for dessert. And they seem so satisfied! Every time, with their virtuous dessert choices, so thoroughly content! I don't really get it. But I have to say, when I came up with this fruit crisp, bursting with exotic spice, I might have begun to take steps toward understanding that kind of lifestyle.

Granted, there's not just fruit here—there is a crisp, granola-like topping going on as well—but with a filling that's entirely fruit-driven and sweetened only with apple juice . . . well, perhaps even I can eventually get down with that whole wacky fruit-for-dessert thing.

FILLING

One 12-ounce (340 grams) can frozen unsweetened apple juice concentrate, thawed

4 cardamom pods

2 star anise

1 cinnamon stick, broken in half

½ vanilla bean, split lengthwise

Pinch of fine sea salt

2 tablespoons plus ½ teaspoon (½ ounce/15 grams) cornstarch

4 medium firm-ripe Bartlett pears, peeled, cored, and cut into 1-inch chunks

4 medium Granny Smith apples, peeled, cored, and cut into 1-inch chunks

2 teaspoons freshly squeezed lemon juice

12 ounces (340 grams) fresh blackberries

1. Position a rack in the lower third of the oven and preheat the oven to 350°F. Lightly grease a 9 × 13-inch glass or ceramic baking dish with butter or nonstick cooking spray.

2. Make the filling: In a medium saucepan, combine the apple juice concentrate, cardamom pods, star anise, cinnamon stick, vanilla bean, and salt. Set the pan over high heat and bring the liquid to a rapid boil. Boil for 1 minute. Remove the pan from the heat, cover the pan, and let steep for 30 minutes. Strain the juice, discarding the spices.

3. In a small bowl, whisk together 2 tablespoons of the spiced juice with the cornstarch until dissolved. Pour the rest of the juice back into the saucepan and bring it back to a boil over medium-high heat. Whisk in the cornstarch mixture and continue whisking until thickened and syrupy, about 1 minute. Remove the pan from the heat.

When you use gluten-free oats, this dessert becomes not only free of refined sugars but gluten- and dairy-free, too.

CRISP TOPPING

2 large egg whites, at room temperature

6 tablespoons (4½ ounces/126 grams) honey

¼ cup (2⅝ ounces/76 grams) grapeseed, vegetable, or coconut oil

1 teaspoon pure vanilla extract

½ teaspoon fine sea salt

4 cups (14 ounces/400 grams) old-fashioned rolled oats

½ cup (1¾ ounces/50 grams) almond meal or finely ground almonds

Turbinado sugar, for sprinkling (optional)

4. In a large bowl, combine the pears and apples. Pour in the lemon juice and toss, rubbing the lemon juice into the fruit pieces. Add the blackberries to the bowl. Pour the spiced apple syrup over the fruit, and using a large flexible spatula, stir gently to combine. Scrape the fruit into the prepared pan, spreading it evenly.

5. Make the crisp topping: In another large bowl, whisk together the egg whites, honey, oil, vanilla extract, and salt until smooth. Add the oats and almond meal or ground almonds and stir until the oats are evenly moistened. Dump the topping onto the fruit and spread gently with your hands so that the crisp topping is in an even layer but not compacted. Sprinkle the top with turbinado sugar for extra sparkle and crunch, if you like.

6. Bake until the crisp is browned and the fruit is tender and bubbling, about 1 hour. Set the crisp to cool on a wire rack for at least 30 minutes before serving.

TIP: *Be sure to set your oven rack in the lower third of your oven—the top will begin to burn if the crisp bakes in a higher position.*

Everything Autumn Muffins

MAKES 1 DOZEN MUFFINS

When it comes to using more natural sugars in baking, the best place to start is with recipes that you really know and adore. So it makes perfect sense that I asked Matt Lewis and Renato Poliafito, who own the phenomenal Baked bakery in Brooklyn, to let me play with their (already-perfect) Pumpkin Chocolate Chip Loaf recipe for this book. This version turns the loaf into nutty, streusel-topped muffins that have a good punch of whole wheat. With loads of pumpkin, maple, apple chunks, and warming spices, these little babies are all things autumn, in muffin form.

MUFFINS

1½ cups (6⅜ ounces/180 grams) whole wheat pastry flour, spooned and leveled

1½ teaspoons ground cinnamon

1 teaspoon baking soda

1 teaspoon fine sea salt

¼ teaspoon freshly ground nutmeg

¼ teaspoon ground ginger

¾ cup plus 2 tablespoons (7½ ounces/212 grams) pumpkin puree*

¾ cup (8⅞ ounces/252 grams) pure maple syrup

½ cup (4 ounces/113 grams) canola or grapeseed oil

2 large eggs

1 teaspoon pure vanilla extract

1 medium Granny Smith apple, peeled, cored, and diced into ¼-inch pieces**

STREUSEL

9 tablespoons (2½ ounces/72 grams) whole wheat pastry flour, spooned and leveled

3 tablespoons (1⅜ ounces/38 grams) turbinado sugar

⅛ teaspoon fine sea salt

3 tablespoons (1½ ounces/43 grams) cold unsalted butter, cut into ½-inch pieces

⅓ cup (1⅜ ounces/38 grams) chopped pecans

*This is equal to about half of a 15-ounce can of solid-pack pumpkin (look for 100% pure pumpkin puree—not pumpkin pie filling!).

**If you're feeling indulgent, swap out the apple chunks for ¾ cup (4½ ounces/128 grams) bittersweet chocolate chips (60% to 70% cacao).

1. Position a rack in the center of the oven and preheat the oven to 400°F. Line a 12-cup muffin tin with paper liners.

2. Make the muffins: In a large bowl, whisk together the flour, cinnamon, baking soda, salt, nutmeg, and ginger.

3. In a medium bowl, whisk together the pumpkin puree, maple syrup, oil, eggs, and vanilla extract until very smooth.

4. Fold in the apple chunks.

5. Make a well in the center of the dry ingredients and pour in the wet mixture. Fold gently until well blended. Let the batter rest for 10 minutes.

6. Make the streusel: In a medium bowl, whisk together the flour, sugar, and salt. Add the butter and stir with a fork, using the tines of the fork to lightly toss and break up the mixture into crumbles as the dough comes together. Stir in the pecans.

7. Fill the wells of the muffin tin about three-quarters full of batter. Sprinkle a generous tablespoonful of streusel over each muffin. Bake for 20 to 25 minutes, or until a toothpick inserted into the center of several muffins comes out clean. Let the muffins cool for just a couple of minutes in the pan before removing them to a wire rack to cool completely.

TIP: *These muffins are a make-ahead wonder: they're even better—more moist, more full of spice and pumpkin flavor—the day after baking. They also freeze beautifully.*

An Ode to Whole Wheat Pastry Flour

For the longest time, I was an all-or-nothing type person when it came to desserts. "Give me cake or give me death!"—that sort of thing. And generally speaking, I'd still rather go without dessert than eat something "healthy" that's masquerading as cake. That business makes me twitch.

As you've probably noticed, I don't believe in cutting out all the butter or using artificial ingredients to reduce calories, but my feeling is that if you can make an ingredient swap, benefit from it, and not even know it's there or make the whole thing taste even better, why the heck not? (And hey, black beans in brownies—*we totally know you're there*.) But ever since I started treat making with more natural sweeteners, I've also been incorporating other less refined baking ingredients that complement Real Sweets.

Take whole wheat pastry flour, for instance. This has got to be one of the easiest swaps to make to inject a little more health into your baked goods. It's basically very finely milled whole wheat flour, made from soft wheat, and lower in gluten than both stone-ground whole wheat and all-purpose flours. So you get all the great nutrients of whole wheat without your baked goods coming out like doorstops. I use a lot of whole wheat pastry flour in this book and continue to experiment with it in other recipes. Here are a few tips for working with this awesome ingredient.

Sturdy recipes that aren't very airy and have a lot of liquid or fat in them, such as muffins and quick breads, tend to be the best candidates for a full swap of white all-purpose flour to whole wheat pastry flour. Some cookies, waffles, pancakes, brownies, bar cookies, and pie crust (with a few secret tweaks, see page 245) can also take this flour well.

Whole wheat pastry flour tends to absorb more liquid than all-purpose overall, but it takes time to hydrate because of the additional fiber. Let batters and doughs rest for 10 to 20 minutes before baking, and if it's a recipe such as pie dough that already calls for resting, increase the rest time by at least 50 percent.

Because it can be drying, it's especially important not to overload your measuring cup when measuring whole wheat pastry flour by volume. The recipes in this book use a "spooned and leveled" cup of flour that's on the lighter side (4¼ ounces/120 grams). To make sure your cup of flour isn't too heavy, first aerate the container of flour by stirring it with a knife, then spoon it into the cup and level off the cup with the back of a knife.

To further combat dryness, try reducing the amount of whole wheat pastry flour in a white flour recipe by a tablespoon or increasing the liquid by a tablespoon for every cup of flour.

Avoid overbaking when using whole wheat pastry flour—pull the baked goods from the oven a couple minutes early when in doubt.

If I'm using whole wheat pastry flour in a white flour recipe for the first time, I start with a half-and-half mix of all-purpose and whole wheat pastry flours, see what happens, and adjust the ratio gradually from there.

Certain recipes will come out a little heavier when made with whole wheat pastry flour and lose their all-purpose flour magic (like super-light cakes, for instance)—that's just the nature of the whole wheat beast. Sometimes it's just not worth the swap, even after a lot of experimenting. But if I'm working with a recipe that needs additional lightness, such as whole wheat pie pastry, I'll add some baking powder (about ¼ teaspoon per cup of flour) and/or some cornstarch (1 tablespoon for each cup of whole wheat pastry flour), and get a wonderful result.

With its natural subtle nutty flavor, whole wheat pastry flour is especially awesome for savory baked goods.

It can be hard to find in some supermarkets, so I look for whole wheat pastry flour in natural foods stores and buy it in bulk for the best price.

Because it has more oils in it than all-purpose flour, whole wheat flours can go rancid within a couple months at room temperature. For longer-term storage, keep whole wheat pastry flour in the freezer (measure out the amount you need for a recipe, spread it out on a plate or baking sheet, and let it come to room temperature before using it).

CHAPTER 4

Candies and Confections

IS THERE ANYTHING MORE GLORIOUS and glee-inducing than candy? In a health-obsessed world, there's just something awesome about recipes that are unabashedly reliant on copious amounts of sugar. While one can often successfully trim the sweet stuff from all sorts of cakes, cookies, and creams, candy laughs at you when you try to de-sugar it. Candy is the epito-me of "treat"—something to be eaten and savored only every now and again to reap its full day-brightening benefits—and in my opinion should be celebrated for the sugar bomb that it is. But there's no reason that we can't make the good even better. It just so happens that there's no better way to elevate candies and confections than by swapping out white sugar for a variety of flavorful natural sugars that sweeten (and season!) with a variety of complex flavors.

Pomegranate Candied Apples

MAKES 6 MEDIUM TO LARGE APPLES

Irresistible in that nostalgic, stick-to-your-molars sort of way, these candied apples are the type with a shiny hard candy shell. And thanks to a good dose of unsweetened pomegranate juice, this version actually has great flavor beyond just being sweet as well as a beautiful red tinge to the gleaming coating without using buckets of artificial food coloring.

6 medium to large firm sweet-tart apples, at room temperature*

2 cups (16 ounces/454 grams) pure unsweetened pomegranate juice

1½ cups (10½ ounces/300 grams) evaporated cane juice

½ cup (6 ounces/168 grams) brown rice syrup

1 cinnamon stick, broken in half

¼ teaspoon fine sea salt

* I like tart Granny Smith apples for candying, or something slightly sweeter, such as the Pink Lady variety. Don't use apples straight out of the fridge, or their candy coats won't go on smoothly. Unwaxed, organic apples are the best choice.

1. Insert a sturdy wooden skewer or Popsicle stick into the stem end of each apple and set them aside. Line a large baking sheet with parchment paper or aluminum foil and grease it lightly with neutral-tasting oil or spray it with nonstick cooking spray, or use a silicone baking mat.

2. In a large (4-quart) heavy-bottomed saucepan, combine the pomegranate juice, evaporated cane juice, brown rice syrup, cinnamon stick, and salt. Set the pan over medium-high heat and stir gently to combine until the syrup reaches a boil. Clip a candy thermometer onto the side of the pan. Cook the syrup to 285°F. Be prepared to pull the pan from the heat as soon as it hits 285°F—the fruit juice will burn and darken quickly after this point. Using the tines of a fork, carefully fish the cinnamon stick out of the syrup and discard it.

3. Working quickly with one apple at a time, plunge the apple into the candy, submerging it all the way to the top of the fruit. Avoid the temptation to double dip the apple in the hot candy—it will get thick and goopy instead of leaving the apple with a shatteringly thin, shiny coat.

TIP: *If you can find thin wooden dowels or thick bamboo skewers to use as sticks, you can dress up the apples by slipping a fun-patterned paper straw over the stick.*

4. Pull the apple out of the pot, allowing any excess syrup to drip off for a brief moment, and then set the apple onto the prepared baking sheet. Repeat the dipping process with the remaining apples. If the candy starts to thicken and becomes hard to work with, just put the pan over a very low flame and stir gently until it's more fluid again. Let the apples cool until the candy has hardened completely, about 30 minutes. Candied apples are best served and eaten soon after they're made.

Cracklin' Maple Popcorn

MAKES ABOUT 2 QUARTS

My love affair with popcorn is serious. It's really the perfect, crunchy blank canvas for so many flavors, from sweet to savory. Sweet and salty caramel corn is an obvious choice, but when you get some natural sweeteners involved, it takes something familiar to the next crave-worthy level. Here maple syrup, molasses, and turbinado sugar play a mean trio, lending lots of rich flavor and color to the caramel and giving you a result that's a whole lot like that classic caramel corn that comes in that iconic red-and-white box, but better. You won't even miss the surprise toy inside.

This recipe is pictured on page 143.

8 cups (2 ounces/57 grams) popped popcorn*

Fine sea salt

½ cup (1⅞ ounces/53 grams) roasted, salted peanuts or coarsely chopped toasted pecans

7 tablespoons (5 ounces/147 grams) pure maple syrup

½ cup (3½ ounces/100 grams) turbinado sugar

¼ cup (2 ounces/57 grams) water

1 tablespoon unsulphured molasses

½ teaspoon pure vanilla extract

¼ teaspoon baking soda

3 tablespoons (1½ ounces/43 grams) unsalted butter, cut into pieces

*Either air-popped or popped in a bit of oil on the stove, ⅓ cup unpopped kernels will yield the amount of popcorn needed here. You can also use unbuttered, lightly salted microwave popcorn (often labeled "natural") in a pinch.

1. Preheat the oven to 250°F. Line a large rimmed baking sheet with a silicone baking mat or butter it generously.

2. Season the popcorn with salt and remove any unpopped kernels. Combine the popcorn with the peanuts or pecans on the prepared baking sheet and keep them warm in the oven while you prepare the sugar syrup.

3. In a medium heavy-bottomed saucepan, stir together the maple syrup, sugar, water, molasses, and ¼ teaspoon of the fine sea salt. Bring the syrup to a boil over high heat—once the syrup is boiling, stop stirring. Clip a candy thermometer to the side of the pan and reduce the heat to medium. Cook the syrup until the temperature reaches 250°F, about 10 minutes. Remove the pan from the heat and stir in the vanilla extract and baking soda. Stir in the butter.

4. Remove the warm pan of popcorn and pecans from the oven and quickly pour the syrup over them in a thin, steady stream. Toss to coat evenly. Spread the coated popcorn into an even layer and bake for 45 minutes, stirring well every 15 minutes, until dry and crisp. Let cool completely and store in an airtight container.

Gingerbread Fudge

MAKES ABOUT 2 DOZEN 1-INCH PIECES

Without a speck of chocolate in the mix, this generously spiced, creamy confection definitely flips the script on the idea of fudge. Far from traditional, this candy is intense—super sweet, rich with molasses flavor and cream. Even cut into tiny squares, this stuff packs a punch. It's the ultimate surprise for tucking into holiday cookie tins.

1½ cups (12 ounces/340 grams) firmly packed dark muscovado sugar

½ cup (4¼ ounces/120 grams) heavy cream

1 tablespoon brown rice syrup

½ teaspoon fine sea salt

1 tablespoon unsalted butter, cut into small pieces

¾ teaspoon ground cinnamon

½ teaspoon ground ginger

½ teaspoon pure vanilla extract

1. Line a 9 × 5-inch loaf pan with aluminum foil, leaving a couple of inches of overhang on the two longer sides of the pan. Lightly spray the foil with nonstick cooking spray, and use a paper towel to wipe away any excess oil in the corners.

2. In a medium heavy-bottomed saucepan, combine the sugar, cream, brown rice syrup, and salt. Place the pan over medium-high heat and stir gently. Once the syrup comes up to a bubble, stop stirring, and clip a candy thermometer onto the side of the pan. Boil until it reaches 240°F. Remove the pan from the heat (don't remove the thermometer!) and stir in the butter, cinnamon, ginger, and vanilla extract until well blended. Set the pan on a heatproof surface and cool the syrup to 110°F, about 30 minutes. Check the thermometer periodically, but do not stir or jostle the pan to prevent sugar crystals from forming (for your stillness, you will be rewarded with a smooth, creamy fudge).

3. Scrape the cooled fudge into the bowl of an electric mixer fitted with the paddle attachment. Beat on medium speed until the fudge thickens considerably, loses most of its gloss, and looks something like warm Silly Putty, about

MUSCOVADO WALNUT FUDGE

Omit the spices and fold in ½ cup (2 ounces/57 grams) chopped toasted walnuts.

10 minutes. (Alternatively, beat with a handheld mixer right in the saucepan). Scrape the fudge into the prepared pan, and with lightly oiled fingertips, press the candy evenly into the pan. Trim a sheet of parchment to fit the pan and lay it over the surface of the fudge; use your hands to smooth the top.

4. Chill in the refrigerator until firm, about 1 hour. Use the foil to remove the fudge slab from the pan and transfer it to a cutting board. Cut into 1-inch squares with a sharp, lightly oiled knife. Store in an airtight container in the refrigerator for up to 2 weeks.

Honeycomb Candy

MAKES ABOUT 1 POUND OF CANDY

Depending on your location, this airy, crunchy, quirky candy is called everything from sponge candy to sea foam to honeycomb. Let's call it honeycomb for the sake of being literal—this version actually uses honey, turning this confection-meets-science-experiment into a powerhouse of flavor and texture.

Make sure you use a large enough pot here—the candy will bubble up really high when the baking soda is added. I use a 5-quart Dutch oven, which seems awkwardly large at first—you'll have to tilt the pan every few minutes so that the thermometer is submerged enough in the syrup to get a proper temperature reading.

1 cup (7 ounces/200 grams) evaporated cane juice

¼ cup (3 ounces/84 grams) honey

¾ cup (9 ounces/255 grams) brown rice syrup

1 tablespoon distilled white vinegar

½ teaspoon fine sea salt

1 tablespoon pure vanilla extract

1 tablespoon baking soda

1 tablespoon unsalted butter

TIP: *When you cut the candy into chunks, you'll get a fair amount of sweet, crunchy shards left behind on the cutting board. Don't be a fool—save these addictive bits for ice cream topping.*

1. Generously spray a 9-inch springform pan with 3-inch-high sides with nonstick cooking spray. Set the prepared pan on a baking sheet.

2. In a large heavy-bottomed pot (such as a 5-quart Dutch oven), combine the evaporated cane juice, honey, brown rice syrup, vinegar, and salt. Stir to combine over medium-high heat. Bring to a boil, and clip a candy thermometer onto the side of the pot. Cook to 295°F, stirring often. Remove the pot from the heat. Stir in the vanilla extract and baking soda and stand back slightly—the candy will bubble and poof up in the pot in the most magical (and slightly dangerous-looking) way. Add the butter and stir until melted. Pour the candy into the prepared pan and let cool, about 1 hour.

3. Unmold the candy slab onto a cutting board. With a large knife, cut the candy into chunks. Store in an airtight container at room temperature for up to 1 week.

Nutty Honey Taffy

MAKES ABOUT 4 DOZEN 1½-INCH PIECES

Danger: highly addictive substance ahead. If you love those old-fashioned, nutty, honey-flavored chews in the red and yellow wrappers, then you'll "bee" a rabid fan of this recipe (sorry, it's the sugar rush talking).

It may seem like a sort of daunting task to make taffy at home, but really it's just like making caramels, with some bonus calorie-burning upper-body exercise. Which is terrific, because about half of the taffy pieces will somehow make their way into your mouth while you wrap them.

This recipe is pictured on page 142.

1 cup (12 ounces/336 grams) honey

1 cup (7 ounces/200 grams) turbinado sugar

¼ cup (2 ounces/57 grams) water

½ teaspoon fine sea salt

2 tablespoons (1 ounce/28 grams) unsalted butter

2 tablespoons (1⅛ ounces/32 grams) almond butter or natural peanut butter (crunchy, salt-added variety)✱

½ teaspoon pure vanilla extract

1 teaspoon apple cider vinegar, white vinegar, or lemon juice

⅛ teaspoon baking soda

✱ Almond butter will bring you a little closer to that aforementioned iconic honey candy.

1. Line a large baking sheet with parchment paper and spray it lightly with nonstick cooking spray, or use a silicone baking mat. Prepare a large, heatproof work surface for pulling, rolling, and cutting the taffy—this could be a length of clean countertop sprayed with nonstick cooking spray, or if you don't have that kind of kitchen real estate, you can simply invert a baking sheet and lay a silicone baking mat on top of it, or spray the back of it with nonstick spray.

2. In a large heavy-bottomed saucepan, stir together the honey, sugar, water, and salt. Place the pot over high heat and stir gently. Once the syrup reaches a bubble, stop stirring and clip a candy thermometer onto the side of the pot. Cook to 270°F.

TIP: *I love using regular old paper cupcake liners for wrapping candies—they're cheap, easy to find, and even come in fun holiday colors. Plus you don't have to cut a bunch of little squares of parchment like a crazy person.*

3. Immediately remove the pan from the heat and whisk in the butter, almond butter, vanilla extract, and vinegar until smooth. Whisk in the baking soda and keep whisking for 1 full minute—the mixture will suddenly become lighter in color and poof up a bit. Pour the candy onto the prepared baking sheet. Let cool at room temperature until cool enough to handle, about 30 minutes.

4. Spray a large sharp knife or kitchen scissors with nonstick spray and divide the taffy into fourths. Spray your hands with nonstick spray. Working with one-quarter of the taffy at a time, grasp it with both hands and pull and stretch the taffy. Fold it back onto itself and pull again. Continue pulling the taffy until it's glossy, lightened in color, and begins to resist pulling, letting you know that it's been properly cooled and aerated. Depending on your strength and speed, this can take anywhere from 10 to 15 minutes, but it's better to err on the side of more time for a lighter, chewier, and less sticky taffy.

5. Place the pulled taffy on the prepared work surface and roll into a rope about 20 inches long and ½ inch in diameter. Cut the rope into pieces about 1½ inches long. Place the cut pieces on a baking sheet (also either lined with a silicone baking mat or prepared with nonstick spray) as you work. Repeat the pulling, rolling, and cutting process with the remaining three quarters of the taffy. Immediately wrap the cut taffy pieces in small parchment squares or in paper cupcake liners. Store in an airtight container in a very cool, very dry place for up to 1 week.

TIP: *In addition to recruiting a couple of friends to help with the pulling, making everything as nonstick as possible is the name of the game here to ensure a fun, easy taffy-making process. Have a can of nonstick cooking spray at the ready for your hands and work surface, and I highly recommend silicone baking mats for candymaking.*

Maple Marshmallows

MAKES TWENTY-FIVE 1½-INCH MARSHMALLOWS

Ever the homemade marshmallow enthusiast (having quite literally written the book on them for my first cookbook), I'm always looking for ways to bump up their flavor. The combination of maple sugar and maple syrup makes for a wonderful, intensely flavored marshmallow. Just imagine the s'mores you could throw down with these babies. Bittersweet chocolate, Homemade Graham Crackers (see page 48), and maple mallows? Call me.

This recipe is pictured on page 143.

4½ teaspoons (⅜ ounce/11 grams) unflavored powdered gelatin✶

3 tablespoons (1½ ounces/43 grams) cold water

2 large egg whites, at room temperature

½ cup (3¼ ounces/92 grams) pure maple sugar

½ cup (6 ounces/168 grams) pure maple syrup

2 tablespoons (1 ounce/28 grams) water

½ teaspoon fine sea salt

1½ teaspoons pure vanilla extract

3 tablespoons (¾ ounce/21 grams) cornstarch

1 tablespoon organic confectioners' sugar

✶ Equal to about 2 envelopes of unflavored gelatin powder—pour the packets into a small bowl and measure them precisely, since the amount in the packets can vary. If you want to use sheets, look for "gold strength" sheets and measure 12 grams by weight.

1. Lightly spray an 8 × 8-inch square baking pan with nonstick cooking spray. Use a paper towel to remove any excess oil that might pool in the edges and corners.

2. In a small bowl, whisk together the gelatin and cold water. Set aside to soften for at least 5 minutes.

3. Into the bowl of an electric mixer fitted with the whisk attachment, add the egg whites. Beat on medium-high speed until soft peaks form, about 3 minutes. Stop the mixer.

4. In a medium saucepan, combine the maple sugar, maple syrup, water, and salt. Stir gently over high heat until the syrup comes up to a boil. Stop stirring, and clip a candy thermometer onto the side of the pan. Cook to 240°F. Immediately pull the pan from the heat and whisk in the lump of softened gelatin until it is completely melted.

TIP: *Your biggest clue that the marshmallow has finished whipping is that the bowl will be cool to the touch all over. Underwhipping the batter leads to damp mallows that are tricky to store.*

5. Turn the mixer back on to medium speed. Slowly begin to drizzle the sugar syrup into the egg whites, just a tablespoon or so at a time at first, to avoid scrambling the whites. Once a few tablespoons have been beaten into the whites, pour in the rest of the syrup, using a heatproof spatula to ensure that all the syrup is scraped into the mixer bowl. Raise the mixer speed to medium-high and beat until the marshmallow is thick, billowing, and glossy, and roughly tripled in volume, and the mixer bowl is cool to the touch all over, about 10 minutes. Beat in the vanilla extract.

6. Pour the marshmallow into the prepared pan and use an offset spatula to nudge it into the corners and smooth the top.

7. To make the coating, into a medium bowl, sift together the cornstarch and confectioners' sugar. Sift the coating evenly and generously over the top of the marshmallow. Let set for at least 6 hours in a cool, dry place.

8. When the marshmallow has set, use a knife to loosen the marshmallow from the edges of the pan. Invert the marshmallow slab onto a coating-dusted work surface and dust it with more coating. Cut into whatever size pieces you wish. Dip the sticky edges of the marshmallows in more coating, patting off the excess.

9. Store in an airtight container for up to 2 weeks.

TIP: *When choosing a saucepan for this recipe, err on the side of something smaller—1½ to 2 quarts should do the trick. If the pan is too large, the level of the sugar syrup will be too low for the tip of the thermometer to be submerged and give an accurate temperature reading.*

Orange Blossom Honey
and Walnut Toffee
(page 146)

Nutty Honey Taffy
(page 138)

Cracklin'
Maple Popcorn
(page 133)

Raw Sugar and
Mascarpone Caramels
(page 144)

Maple Marshmallows
(page 140)

Raw Sugar and Mascarpone Caramels

MAKES ABOUT SIXTY-FOUR 1-INCH SQUARES

Now you might be thinking, *Mascarpone cheese, in caramels? Say what?* But here's the thing: with a fat content similar to butter's, mascarpone is great in some recipes where I want the richness of butter without the, well, buttery-ness, which can sometimes overwhelm the subtle flavors of natural sugars. Here the mascarpone allows the natural caramel notes of turbinado and the round, mellow sweetness of brown rice syrup to come forward, in addition to lending a wonderful creamy chew.

This recipe is pictured on page 143.

1¼ cups (8¾ ounces/248 grams) turbinado sugar

⅓ cup (4 ounces/113 grams) brown rice syrup

¼ cup (2 ounces/57 grams) water

1¼ teaspoons crunchy, flaky sea salt (such as Maldon), plus more for sprinkling

⅔ cup (5⅝ ounces/161 grams) heavy cream, at room temperature

⅓ cup (2⅝ ounces/75 grams) mascarpone cheese, at room temperature

1½ teaspoons pure vanilla extract

1. Line an 8 × 8-inch baking pan with aluminum foil and lightly oil the foil or spray it with nonstick cooking spray. Wipe away any excess that might be beading or pooling in the corners with a paper towel.

2. In a heavy medium saucepan over medium heat, combine the sugar, brown rice syrup, water, and salt. Stirring gently, bring the mixture to a boil over a 5-minute period—you want to give the sugar as much time as you can to dissolve before the syrup begins to boil. Once the sugar is visibly dissolved, raise the heat to medium-high and clip a candy thermometer to the pot. Cook until the caramel reaches 300°F, 5 to 7 minutes. Remove the pan from the heat and remove the thermometer. Carefully pour in the cream and stir until smooth. Place the pan back over medium-high heat and refasten the thermometer to the pan. Boil the caramel again to 260°F, 4 to 5 minutes more. Remove the pan from the heat and stir in the mascarpone cheese and vanilla extract until well blended.

3. Pour the caramel into the prepared baking pan. Set the baking pan over a wire rack and let the caramel cool, undisturbed, until firm, at least 2 hours at room temperature.

4. Line a cutting surface with a sheet of parchment paper and turn the caramel slab out onto it. Use a large sharp knife to cut the caramel into 1-inch squares. Top each caramel with an extra sprinkling of flaky sea salt, if you like. Wrap the caramels in squares of parchment or waxed paper, or paper cupcake liners. Store at room temperature.

TIP: *As appealing as cutting parchment sheets into millions of tiny squares might seem, I prefer buying precut candy wrappers online or using paper cupcake liners for an even cheaper, more convenient option.*

Orange Blossom Honey and Walnut Toffee

MAKES ABOUT 2 POUNDS

I'm a sucker for crunchy, buttery toffee of all kinds, but I'm especially enamored of this version, which features the beautiful flavor of orange blossom honey. The pairing of this ambrosial honey and walnuts is downright sexy, and gives this candy a delightfully unexpected flavor twist. Call it confectionery vanity, but I also choose natural sugars based on the color they'll impart—the combination of coconut sugar and honey here gives the toffee its stunning, deep amber gloss.

This recipe is pictured on page 142.

1 cup (2 sticks/8 ounces/226 grams) unsalted butter, cut into tablespoon-size pieces

1 cup (5¼ ounces/150 grams) coconut sugar

¼ cup (3 ounces/84 grams) orange blossom honey

½ teaspoon fine sea salt

½ teaspoon pure vanilla extract

1 cup (4¼ ounces/120 grams) raw walnuts, chopped

TIP: *This recipe can easily be doubled with great results.*

1. Line a large baking sheet with aluminum foil or a silicone baking mat. Lightly oil the foil, if using.

2. In a medium heavy-bottomed saucepan over medium-low heat, begin melting the butter. When the butter is about three-quarters melted, add the sugar, honey, and salt. Stir gently with a heatproof spatula or wooden spoon. Continue stirring slowly until the sugar has begun to dissolve—the mixture will turn from looking like a separated mess into something much more smooth and homogenous, and it will begin to bubble. Turn the heat up to medium and stir occasionally while the toffee cooks—the bubbling should be sort of groovy and dreamy-looking, not a full, rapid boil. Clip a candy thermometer to the side of the pan, making sure it doesn't touch the bottom of the pot.

3. Continue stirring the candy often to prevent burning until the temperature reads 285°F. Immediately remove the pan from the heat and stir in the vanilla extract and walnuts. Pour the toffee onto the prepared baking sheet. Use a heatproof spatula to pop any bubbles that rise to the surface of the candy while it's still hot. Set the toffee aside to cool for about 30 minutes. Once set, break the toffee into pieces. Store in an airtight container unrefrigerated for up to 5 days, in the refrigerator for 2 weeks, or in the freezer for up to 1 month.

TIP: *The impressive amount of butter in this recipe makes refrigeration or even freezing a good idea if it will be stored for longer than a few days.*

Brigadeiros

MAKES ABOUT 2 DOZEN 1-INCH CANDIES

Somewhere between a fudgy chocolate truffle and a Tootsie Roll is the Brazilian confection known as the *brigadeiro*. The recipe is so dead simple it can hardly be called a recipe, and the possibilities are endless as far as decorating them goes. Traditionally, *brigadeiros* are found with a coating of thin, crunchy chocolate sprinkles, but you can go crazy with fun coatings here—roll the candy balls in cocoa powder, grated chocolate, toasted shredded coconut, or finely chopped nuts of all sorts.

1¼ cups (14 ounces/397 grams) Homemade Sweetened Condensed Milk (see page 228)*****

⅓ cup (1⅛ ounces/32 grams) unsweetened natural cocoa powder

2 tablespoons (1 ounce/28 grams) unsalted butter, cut into small pieces

⅛ teaspoon fine sea salt

¼ teaspoon pure vanilla extract

Chocolate sprinkles,****** grated chocolate, cocoa powder, or other creative coatings

*To fully celebrate the Brazilian heritage of this candy, consider using rapadura to make your sweetened condensed milk. Or, to forgo the step of making your own, swap in one 14-ounce can of store-bought organic sweetened condensed milk. If you use canned milk, the candy is likely to thicken and cook faster, so keep an eye out for the visual cues described below to avoid overcooking it.

1. Lightly grease an 8 × 8-inch baking pan (or another heatproof vessel with approximately the same dimensions) with butter or nonstick cooking spray.

2. In a medium heavy-bottomed saucepan, combine the sweetened condensed milk, cocoa powder, butter, and salt. Place the pan over medium heat and whisk often to encourage the butter to melt and the cocoa powder to dissolve. Once the candy comes to a bubble, reduce the heat to low and cook, whisking often. The candy is finished when it's the consistency of a thick brownie batter and slides in a soft mass from one side of the pan to the other when the pan is tilted—this can take anywhere from 15 to 25 minutes, depending on your stove, but it's better to keep the heat low and give the candy more time to cook down than to rush it and risk burning it. Stir in the vanilla extract. Pour the candy into the prepared baking pan. Chill in the refrigerator until the candy is somewhat firm with a claylike texture, about 1 hour.

** Look for the tasty real deal, such as chocolate vermicelli made by Guittard or Callebaut, rather than the shorter, fatter jimmies made with shortening and other ingredients that have a waxy mouthfeel.

3. When you're ready to form the candies, pour your desired coatings onto individual plates. Use your fingers or a small ice cream scoop with a capacity of about 1 teaspoon to portion out bits of candy and roll them into 1-inch balls. Drop each ball into a dish of coating and roll to coat. Set the finished candies on a small baking sheet, or place them into small paper candy cups. Store in the refrigerator in an airtight container.

A Sticky Wicket

It used to be that I would irrationally panic a bit when faced with measuring out sticky liquid sweeteners like honey, maple syrup, and molasses. The thought of trying to scrape every last bit of sticky stuff into my mixing bowl while simultaneously trying to keep it from traveling onto my hands and into my hair gave me the heebie-jeebies. And then there's the issue of filling the cup or spoon *riiight* to the top, with no spillage. Maybe I'm just spectacularly uncoordinated, but I had to take control and stop the madness. Here's how I now measure the sticky stuff.

Measuring by weight. I highly recommended becoming cozy with a kitchen scale for all your baking, but when it comes to measuring liquid sweeteners, I find a scale to be the key to avoiding insanity. Nearly every liquid sweetener weighs 21 grams (about ¾ ounce) per tablespoon. Do some quick math, and just pour away, right into the bowl or saucepan that requires the syrup. Clean and easy.

Measuring by volume. If you lack a scale or just aren't in the weighing headspace yet as a baker, you can still have a stress-free measuring experience with liquid sweeteners. The secret is nonstick cooking spray. A little spritz on the inside of your measuring cup or spoon makes thick syrups slip right out. No sticky cleanup, no threads of goo, no cursing.

Caramelized Praline Spread

MAKES ABOUT 1 CUP (10 OUNCES/280 GRAMS)

I love Le Pain Quotidien, a restaurant with several international locations. Sadly, San Francisco isn't one of them, so I have to wait until I'm in LA or New York to have their phenomenal Belgian-style baked goods. One thing that always makes it into my carry-on is a jar of their Brunette Organic Hazelnut Spread. It's a highly addictive substance made of caramelized hazelnuts—think Nutella without the chocolate? Or candied peanut butter but with hazelnuts? Hoo boy. To satisfy my long-distance Brunette cravings, I came up with a homemade version using pecans instead of hazelnuts.

½ cup (3½ ounces/100 grams) turbinado sugar

¼ cup (2 ounces/57 grams) firmly packed dark muscovado sugar

¼ cup (2 ounces/57 grams) whole milk

3 tablespoons (1½ ounces/43 grams) unsalted butter, cut into small pieces

¼ teaspoon fine sea salt

1¼ cups (5 ounces/142 grams) chopped pecans

1½ teaspoons pure vanilla extract

1. Line a rimmed baking sheet with a silicone baking mat or parchment paper (if using parchment, lightly grease it with a bit of nonstick cooking spray).

2. In a medium heavy-bottomed saucepan, combine the turbinado sugar, muscovado sugar, milk, butter, and salt. Set the pan over medium-high heat and stir gently with a flexible heatproof spatula until smooth. Stir in the pecans. Bring the mixture to a boil, and clip a candy thermometer to the side of the pan. Stirring often to keep the syrup and bits of pecan from getting trapped behind the thermometer and burning, cook to 240°F. Remove the pan from the heat and stir in the vanilla extract.

3. Continuously stir the praline for 3 to 4 minutes, or until it begins to cool and form a firm but flexible mass, like a ball of dough, and the sugar starts to crystallize. Dump the praline out onto the prepared pan and smash it into an even layer. Allow the praline to cool completely on the sheet pan.

4. Tumble the cooled praline into the bowl of a food processor fitted with the steel blade. Grind it to a paste, about 5 minutes. At first the mixture will look quite powdery and coarse; after 2 minutes the texture will begin to change as the nuts' oils are released and reabsorbed—it will alternately smooth out and cling to the sides of the bowl, then form a ball that spins around a few times, finally smoothing out again. Scrape down the bowl well and process for 1 more minute. Give it a taste and consider an extra dash of salt.

5. Transfer the spread to an airtight container and chill in the refrigerator for about 1 hour; it will firm up as it cools. Store in the refrigerator for up to 1 month.

Evaporated Cane Juice: the sidekick

Weight: 1 cup/7 ounces/200 grams

Characteristics: Neutral sweetness, fine texture, with hints of vanilla and light caramel, a foolproof swap for granulated white sugar, as it's only a couple of steps less refined. Evaporated cane juice makes for a great "co-starring sugar" when another, less refined sugar with a more intense flavor is the main sweetener.

Where it comes from: Evaporated cane juice comes from sugarcane and can also be found labeled as "organic sugar." It's essentially white granulated sugar, minus the bleaching and other final chemical treatments. "Organic confectioners' sugar" is evaporated cane juice that has been ground fine with a starch like tapioca or cornstarch to prevent clumping.

Best uses: As a 1:1 substitute anywhere you'd use white granulated sugar. I like to use evaporated cane juice as a slightly better quality alternative to white granulated sugar for special-occasion, celebration-type cakes and "sometimes foods" such as candies. In these kinds of recipes, this sugar is used more like a tool than a flavor booster. Its fine texture helps aerate eggs and butter when using in conjunction with liquid sweeteners, which can provide flavor and moisture, but not much loft or structure (as in the Five-Flavors Party Cake on page 178).

Just like white sugar, evaporated cane juice has neutral sweetness that lets other flavors shine. Evaporated cane juice is slightly coarser than regular granulated, so it adds a little more sparkle than regular granulated sugar when used as a topping for muffins, quick breads, and cookies.

Bonus points: When it comes to the natural-sugars pantry, evaporated cane juice definitely is the most refined sugar used in this book and has minimal benefits in terms of nutritional value. But it is closer to its natural state than white granulated cane sugar, and it also is a 100 percent vegan alternative to white cane sugars, many of which get their snow-white color from being filtered through bone char. Bone char is also called "natural charcoal" by large sugar companies and is made from charred animal bones, therefore technically making sugar filtered with it nonvegan.

How to store: Store in a tightly sealed jar in a dry place.

Birdseed Brittle

MAKES ABOUT 1 POUND OF CANDY

At first glance, this candy might look more like one of those childhood projects crafted at school or summer camp to attract our feathered friends. So it's really no surprise that this sweet-salty, brown buttery toffee enrobing a mind-boggling amount of crunchy, earthy seeds of all sorts acts like a bird feeder for the human set. One bite of this unusual little confection will have you flapping your way back to the candy dish, over and over.

1¾ cups (12⅜ ounces/350 grams) turbinado sugar

¼ cup (3 ounces/84 grams) brown rice syrup

½ cup water (4 ounces/113 grams)

1 teaspoon fine sea salt

3 tablespoons (1 ounce/30 grams) pepitas (raw pumpkin seeds)✱

3 tablespoons (1 ounce/30 grams) roasted salted or unsalted sunflower seeds

1 teaspoon white sesame seeds

1 teaspoon chia seeds or black sesame seeds

4 tablespoons (2 ounces/57 grams) unsalted butter, cut into small pieces

½ teaspoon pure vanilla extract

1 teaspoon baking soda

✱ These seed amounts are pretty tiny—I tend to buy my seeds in bulk at natural foods stores so I can get smaller amounts as needed. Use whatever combination of seeds you like!

1. Line a large baking sheet with a silicone baking mat, or line it with parchment and spray it with nonstick cooking spray.

2. In a medium saucepan set over medium-high heat, combine the sugar, brown rice syrup, water, and salt. Stir gently until the syrup begins to boil. Clip a candy thermometer onto the side of the pan. Cook the syrup, stirring occasionally, until it reaches 290°F.

3. While the syrup is boiling, in a small bowl, mix together the pepitas, sunflower seeds, white sesame seeds, and chia seeds or black sesame seeds.

4. When the syrup reaches 290°F, remove the pan from the heat. Stir in the butter and vanilla extract. Once the butter has melted, stir in the baking soda—the mixture will foam up and bubble. Immediately spread the mixture out onto the prepared baking sheet.

5. Spread the candy into a rough rectangle about 8 × 10 inches in size. Sprinkle the seeds over the top. When the candy is still warm and pliable but cool enough to touch, use your palms to press the seeds into the surface of the brittle. Let cool completely before breaking into charmingly irregular hunks.

SPICY BIRDSEED BRITTLE

Omit the vanilla extract and add ⅛ teaspoon of hot chili powder or cayenne pepper (or more, if you dare!) when you whisk in the butter.

Maple Spun Sugar

MAKES 4 TO 6 SOFTBALL-SIZE CLOUDS OF CANDY

I'll admit it—this stuff is ridiculous. It's whimsical, it's beautiful, and it also has a little bit of that "Who would even do that at home?" quality. In short, it's the ultimate party trick. It's also a whole lot of fun once you get the hang of it. After forming the strands, you can either shape them into clouds and pop them onto sticks, or wind them around a plated dessert (like the Piloncillo Dessert Waffles with Caramel Cream and Pan-Roasted Bananas on page 169), and prepare to impress.

SYRUP

1¼ cups (8¾ ounces/250 grams) turbinado sugar

1¼ cups (8⅛ ounces/230 grams) maple sugar

½ cup (6 ounces/168 grams) pure maple syrup or brown rice syrup

½ cup (4 ounces/113 grams) water

⅛ teaspoon fine sea salt

½ teaspoon pure vanilla extract

SPECIAL EQUIPMENT

Long-handled wooden spoons, skewers, or thin wooden dowels

A heavy wooden cutting board, pastry board, or a couple of large books

Newspapers

2 forks

Large bowl of ice water

Cornstarch

1. Begin by preparing the space in which you'll be spinning your sugar: Clear a large, flat work surface, like a countertop or large table. Gather 2 or 3 long-handled wooden spoons, dowels, or thick skewers and lay them on the edge of the countertop with at least 10 inches of overhang. Weigh the sticks down with something heavy you don't mind getting sugar syrup on—some old large books, a hefty wooden cutting board, or a marble pastry board works well. Cover the entire floor area underneath the sticks, and then some, with newspaper (err on the side of more coverage, and if you have cabinetry underneath your work surface, tape some paper onto it as well). Spray the sticks with nonstick cooking spray. Have 2 forks ready for drizzling the syrup. Place a large bowl of ice water near your work space—flinging hot sugar syrup is dangerous stuff!

2. To make the sugar syrup, in a medium (3-quart) heavy-bottomed saucepan, combine the turbinado sugar, maple sugar, maple syrup, water, and salt. Place the pan over medium-high heat and stir gently with a wooden spoon or heatproof spatula to encourage the sugar to dissolve.

Once the syrup comes to a boil, stop stirring. Clip a candy thermometer onto the side of the pan and increase the heat to high. Cook the syrup to 310°F. Immediately pull the pan from the heat and stir in the vanilla extract. Grip the handle of the pan with a gloved hand if the handle isn't heatproof.

3. Take the 2 forks and hold them back-to-back. Stir the syrup gently with the forks to encourage it to cool a bit, then carry the pan over to your sugar-spinning setup. Pull the forks up out of the syrup and hold them about 12 inches over the pan. Examine the way the syrup falls back into the pan—when the syrup has thickened to a honeylike consistency and you can see a spiderweb-like thread or two flying off to the sides, the sugar is ready to spin. Swing the forks back and forth over the sticks, about 10 inches above them. At first, it won't look like much, but soon sugary strands will accumulate, and you'll get the hang of where and how to hold the forks and how fast to swing them in order to get the most control over your sugar.

4. Keep spinning the sugar until you've created about the same amount of strands as shown in the photo opposite. Set down your forks and saucepan and dust your hands very lightly with cornstarch, clapping them like a gymnast to remove any excess. Beginning at the end of one side of the sugar strands, carefully gather them and begin rolling them up toward the sticks. Gently lift the strands as you continue to roll up the cloud of spun sugar, winding down the second side of the sticks, until all the sugar strands have been collected. Softly holding the ball of spun sugar like a baby chick, gently form it into a cloud using the heat of your hands. Insert a bamboo skewer or long lollipop stick into the spun sugar. Continue spinning the sugar with the remaining syrup, rewarming it on the stove over low heat as needed to keep it fluid.

5. Spun sugar is best served very soon after it's made, but you can get a couple hours of life out of it by carefully cloaking each cloud with a plastic bag and tying it with twine around the stick to enclose it and keep it cool and dry.

TIP: *You can double the syrup for this recipe, but I find that smaller batches of syrup are easier to work with. Either way, you can gently rewarm the syrup over low heat as needed to keep it fluid.*

TIP: *Jazz up the candy clouds by inserting plain bamboo or lollipop sticks into fun paper straws.*

Bonfire Toffee Lollipops

MAKES ABOUT 1 DOZEN 2-INCH LOLLIPOPS

Bonfire toffee is a British tradition, and absolutely delicious. Even though it's a total sugar bomb, the hit of bittersweet molasses really rounds out the sweetness and turns it into something really special. You can bump up the molasses flavor even more by swapping out the turbinado sugar for dark muscovado. This toffee can be made in a slab, simply poured into an oiled baking pan, cooled, and broken into pieces, or poured into molds for sweet little lollies.

¾ cup (5¼ ounces/150 grams) turbinado sugar

⅓ cup (4 ounces/113 grams) unsulphured molasses

3 tablespoons (2¼ ounces/63 grams) brown rice syrup

6 tablespoons (3 ounces/85 grams) unsalted butter

¼ teaspoon fine sea salt

¼ teaspoon cream of tartar

TIP: *There are tons of fun lollipop molds available in baking supply shops and online. I love old-fashioned steel molds that look like shallow cookie cutters, which you lay flat on a lined baking sheet and then fill. I also use silicone ice cube trays: just fill the cavities, wait about 15 minutes for the candy to firm up a bit, and then insert the sticks so they'll stay upright. Just make sure your mold is heatproof, and lightly grease it for nonstick insurance.*

1. Have ready a heatproof lollipop mold sprayed with nonstick cooking spray and fitted with lollipop sticks.

2. To make the toffee, measure all the ingredients into a medium heavy-bottomed saucepan. Place the pan over medium heat and stir occasionally until the butter is melted and the sugar has dissolved. Raise the heat to medium-high and bring the candy to a boil. Clip a candy thermometer onto the side of the pan and cook until the temperature reaches 285°F. Immediately remove the pan from the heat.

3. When the candy reaches 285°F, immediately (and carefully!) pour it into lollipop molds with sticks in place. If the candy starts to firm up on you before you can get it all into the molds, simply place the pan back over a very low flame to warm it again. Let the candy harden completely before popping the lollies out of their molds. Wrap the lollipops in clear cellophane as soon as possible (air exposure will make them sticky!).

CHAPTER 5

Dinner Party Fancies

CLIMBING KILIMANJARO. CHILDBIRTH. Throwing your first dinner party and presenting a celebratory dessert to a roomful of oohs and aahs. I'm talking about dealing with adversity and arriving at the other side with a great triumph of the human spirit, people. For me, the ultimate dinner party or celebratory dessert has a touch of fancy flair, great visual appeal, and gives the impression that you have been extremely invested in the preparation of said dessert. So that's what we're going to get into in these next pages.

And I only wish I could be there, to see you in all your glory, leaning over your guests and placing the cake stand in the center of the table with languorous ease, blowing minds and taking names. You've got this.

TIP: *A thin, flexible fish spatula is one of my favorite investments and so useful for any kitchen task that involves delicate foods. It's especially good here because the thin chocolate cake layers are more fragile than your standard breakfast pancake.*

Black-and-White Pancake Cake

SERVES 8 TO 10

Talk about a showstopper! A stack of traditional flapjacks with butter and syrup is fabulous enough as is, but here we're taking that idea into mind-blowing dessert territory. Maple-sweetened chocolate cake batter is cooked up like pancakes into thin layers and then sandwiched with lots of maple cream that beckons for a covert finger swipe. A few hidden slicks of bittersweet chocolate ganache add a major swoon factor to this over-the-top sweet stack.

PANCAKE LAYERS

1 batch of Maple Chocolate Cake batter (see page 101)

½ cup (4 ounces/113 grams) water

CREAM FILLING

½ cup (4¼ ounces/120 grams) heavy cream, chilled

½ cup (4 ounces/113 grams) mascarpone cheese, at room temperature

1½ tablespoons (1⅛ ounces/32 grams) pure maple syrup (dark or very dark preferred)*

1 teaspoon vanilla bean paste or pure vanilla extract

GANACHE FILLING

5 ounces (142 grams) bittersweet chocolate (60% to 70% cacao), chopped

6 tablespoons (3 ounces/85 grams) heavy cream

SPECIAL EQUIPMENT

A cast-iron griddle, about 10 × 17 inches in size**

A very thin, flexible metal spatula, such as a fish spatula

1. Preheat a griddle over low heat for at least 10 minutes. (You want the griddle nice and hot over as low heat as possible to avoid burning the pancakes and to give them ample time to cook through.)

2. Make the pancakes: Whip up a batch of Maple Chocolate Cake, adding the water to the wet ingredients before whisking the batter until smooth.

3. Spray the griddle generously with nonstick spray. Making 2 pancakes at a time, pour two ½-cup scoops of batter onto the griddle. Use the back of a spoon to gently swirl and coax the pancakes into 7-inch circles. Cook the pancakes until the edges appear dry and set and bubbles are no longer popping on the surfaces, about 4 minutes on the first side. Use a thin, flexible metal spatula to gently flip the pancakes. Cook about 2 minutes more, or until the centers of the pancakes spring back when lightly

*With all the chocolate power in this recipe, using the darkest maple syrup in the cake and the filling will help the maple flavor come forward a little more.

**You can also use a very large heavy-bottomed skillet; you'll just have to cook the pancakes one at a time, and the cooking time may vary.

touched. Remove the layers to wire racks to cool completely. Repeat the batter scooping and cooking process until you have 8 cake layers.

4. Line 2 large baking sheets with parchment paper and place 4 cake layers in a single layer on each sheet. Chill in the refrigerator for 10 to 15 minutes.

5. Make the cream filling: Pour the cream into a medium bowl. Whip the cream on high speed to stiff peaks. In a separate medium bowl, place the mascarpone, maple syrup, and vanilla bean paste. Beat on low speed, just until the mixture is smooth and begins to thicken, about 30 seconds—don't overbeat, or the mascarpone will seize. Gently fold in the whipped cream until smooth.

6. Make the ganache filling: Combine the bittersweet chocolate with the cream in a small heatproof bowl. Microwave on high power for 45 to 60 seconds. Whisk the ganache until the chocolate is melted and the ganache is smooth and has the texture of chocolate pudding. Remove about 2 tablespoons of ganache to a small bowl and set aside for garnish.

7. To assemble the cake, remove the pancake layers from the refrigerator. Inspect the layers; choose the most handsome to be the top layer and set it aside. Place 1 cake layer on a serving platter or cake stand. Dollop on ⅓ cup of the maple mascarpone cream and use a small offset spatula to smooth it out, with a ½-inch border all around. Place a second layer on top, and press lightly to help it adhere. Spread about 2½ tablespoons of ganache onto the layer, also with a ½-inch border around the cake. Continue the layering process 6 more times, alternating maple mascarpone cream and chocolate ganache with the layers, placing the best-looking cake layer on top.

8. To the remaining chocolate ganache, add a drizzle of cream, only about ½ teaspoon or so, just enough to thin it to a honeylike consistency (warm the ganache in the microwave for about 10 seconds or so to loosen it up first, if necessary). Drizzle the ganache artfully over the cake. Chill the cake for about 30 minutes before serving. This cake can be made up to 1 day in advance (let it soften on the counter for 15 minutes before slicing).

TIP: *Be prepared to lower the heat accordingly if the pancakes are threatening to burn—just as with making regular breakfast pancakes, depending on your griddle and your stove, it may take a bit of adjusting to get the heat just right. Making a tiny test pancake before cooking the rest of the layers can let you know if you're on the right track.*

Honeyed Yogurt Cheesecake

MAKES ONE 9-INCH CAKE

The cardinal rules of cheesecake making will lead to success here: have all your ingredients at room temperature before you begin, to ensure a lump-free batter; rotate the cake a couple of times during baking; and don't overbake the cake. Any type of honey will work here, but this recipe really lets stronger honeys shine; so if you have access to bold or flavored local honey, this is a great way to use it.

4 large eggs, separated, at room temperature

¼ teaspoon fine sea salt

¼ cup (1¾ ounces/50 grams) evaporated cane juice

3 tablespoons (⅞ ounce/24 grams) unbleached all-purpose flour

1 pound (16 ounces/454 grams) full-fat cream cheese, at room temperature

⅓ cup (4 ounces/113 grams) honey

1 tablespoon freshly squeezed lemon juice

1½ teaspoons pure vanilla extract

1 teaspoon finely grated lemon zest

½ cup (4¼ ounces/120 grams) 2% Greek yogurt, at room temperature

1. Position a rack in the center of the oven and preheat it to 325°F. Lightly spray an 8-inch springform pan with 3-inch-high sides with nonstick cooking spray.

2. In the bowl of an electric mixer fitted with the whisk attachment, place the egg whites and salt. Beat on medium-high speed to soft peaks, 2 to 3 minutes. With the mixer running, slowly rain in the evaporated cane juice. Increase the mixer speed to high and beat until the egg whites are glossy and hold stiff peaks, about 2 minutes. Sift the flour over the whipped whites and gently fold until smooth. Scrape the meringue into a clean bowl. (And hey, guess what? You just made a small batch of angel food cake batter!)

3. Into the mixer bowl (no need to clean it), place the cream cheese. Place the bowl back on the mixer and fit the mixer with the paddle attachment. Beat on medium speed until creamy. Add the honey and beat until smooth. Beat in the egg yolks one at a time. Add the lemon juice, vanilla extract, and lemon zest. Beat to blend well. Reduce the mixer speed to low and stir in the yogurt.

4. Carefully fold about a third of the egg whites into the batter to lighten it. Gently fold in the remaining whites until the batter is smooth. Scrape the batter into the prepared pan.

5. Bake until the cake is puffed, lightly golden, and mostly set, but with a slight wobble when the pan is jostled, 45 to 50 minutes (a toothpick won't tell you much about its doneness; best just to rely on visuals here). Turn off the oven and let the cake cool in the oven for 1 hour. Cover and chill in the refrigerator for at least 3 hours before unmolding the cake and serving.

TIP: *Though this cheesecake is perfectly elegant in its simplicity, you can easily dress it up by topping it with some honey-sweetened whipped cream, or spooning over a batch of the cherry topping from the Chocolate, Cherry, and Cacao Nib Pavlova on page 182.*

Piloncillo Dessert Waffles with Caramel Cream and Pan-Roasted Bananas

SERVES 8

We've all seen those behemoth waffles at diners, piled high with fruit and cream. Nothing wrong with the occasional dessert for breakfast, as far as I'm concerned. But I'm also into flipping the script and doing breakfast for dessert to add a little whimsy to a dinner party or celebration. The waffle base for this dessert is inspired by Liège waffles, those Belgian wonders with hunks of molten pearl sugar crusting the edges.

WAFFLES

1 cup (4½ ounces/128 grams) unbleached all-purpose flour, spooned and leveled

1 teaspoon baking powder

¼ teaspoon baking soda

¼ teaspoon fine sea salt

⅔ cup (5⅝ ounces/160 grams) well-shaken buttermilk

2 large eggs, separated

¼ cup (2 ounces/57 grams) water

2 tablespoons (1 ounce/28 grams) grapeseed or canola oil

1 teaspoon pure vanilla extract

1 cup (4½ ounces/128 grams) piloncillo, chopped into shards and ¼-inch bits*

PAN-ROASTED BANANAS

3 medium firm-ripe bananas, cut into ½-inch-thick slices

1 tablespoon unsalted butter

CARAMEL CREAM AND ASSEMBLY

1 cup (8½ ounces/240 grams) heavy cream, chilled

⅓ cup (3⅜ ounces/95 grams) Buttermilk Caramel Sauce (see page 225), plus extra for drizzling

* You'll need 1 full 4½- to 5-ounce cone of piloncillo for this amount. To make chopping easier, first warm the cone of sugar in the microwave for about 20 seconds on high power. Grab it carefully (an oven mitt comes in handy if the cone gets especially hot!), and hack it up on a cutting board using a large sharp knife.

1. Preheat the oven to 200°F. Set a wire rack over a baking sheet and place it in the oven. Preheat a Belgian-style waffle iron to medium heat. Spray it lightly with nonstick cooking spray.

2. Make the waffles: In a large bowl, whisk together the flour, baking powder, baking soda, and salt.

3. In a medium bowl, whisk together the buttermilk, egg yolks, water, oil, and vanilla extract.

4. Place the egg whites in a separate medium bowl, and using a handheld electric mixer, whip the egg whites to stiff peaks.

5. Pour the buttermilk mixture into the dry ingredients and whisk until smooth. Gently fold in the egg whites with a large flexible spatula. Fold in the chopped piloncillo and any sugary dust that's on the board from chopping. Using a standard ice cream scoop, drop the batter onto the waffle iron in ¼-cup portions, making sure you get plenty of sugary nuggets in each waffle. Cook until the waffles are crisp and deeply golden, and the bits of piloncillo are molten and bubbling, about 4 minutes, depending on your waffle iron. Remove the waffles to the warm oven, arranging them in a single layer. Repeat the waffle-making process with the remaining batter until you have 8 finished waffles.

6. Prepare the bananas: Heat a 10-inch skillet over medium-high heat. Melt the butter in the skillet. Lay the banana slices in a single layer in the hot skillet and let them brown without moving them, turning them once with a thin, flexible metal spatula (a fish spatula is especially good for this), about 1½ minutes per side. Carefully remove the banana slices to paper toweling.

7. Make the caramel cream: In a medium bowl, combine the cream and caramel sauce. Whip the cream to soft peaks.

8. To assemble the waffles, place each waffle on a dessert plate. Dollop a generous ¼ cup of caramel cream atop each waffle. Divide the banana slices equally among the plates and drizzle each waffle with Buttermilk Caramel Sauce.

Maple Cream, Chocolate, and Walnut Tart

MAKES ONE 9-INCH TART

The stars here are the maple cream filling and a salty-sweet graham crust studded with walnuts. The slightest slick of bittersweet chocolate in the bottom of the crust makes for the greatest little surprise, and it's functional: when set, the chocolate helps to keep the crust crisp, and it also just happens to add texture and a dynamite flash of flavor.

CRUST

2 ounces (57 grams) bittersweet chocolate (60% to 70% cacao), melted

2 tablespoons (1 ounce/28 grams) heavy cream

1 Nutty Graham Crust (see page 240), made with maple syrup, baked and cooled completely

FILLING

Batch of Maple Cloud Pudding (see page 219)

TOPPING

½ cup (4¼ ounces/120 grams) heavy cream, chilled

2 teaspoons pure maple syrup

¼ teaspoon pure vanilla extract

Chocolate shavings and toasted chopped walnuts, for sprinkling

1. In a small heatproof bowl, combine the chocolate and cream. Melt together in the microwave with 30-second bursts of high power, stirring well after each interval, until the ganache is smooth.

2. Prepare the crust: Leaving the cooled crust in the tart pan, smooth the melted ganache over the bottom of the crust. Chill in the refrigerator to completely set the ganache, 20 to 30 minutes.

3. Prepare the Maple Cloud Pudding: Right after folding in the whipped cream, smooth the filling into the crust before it has a chance to set. Chill until the filling is set, about 1 hour.

4. Make the topping: Whip the cream with the maple syrup and vanilla extract to soft peaks. Dollop the cream onto the center of the tart and sprinkle the whole thing with chocolate shavings and chopped walnuts.

TIP: *The crust can be baked and slicked with chocolate up to 1 day ahead, but the filling must be prepared right before adding it to the crust and giving the tart a final chill, as it sets up quickly.*

Pistachio Sponge Cake with Honey Cream and Citrus

MAKES ONE 8-INCH CAKE

This recipe is a hybrid of several of my favorite desserts. It's mainly inspired by a Greek treat called *revani*, a butter cake made with ground almonds and soaked in a sweet honey syrup. But I'm a sucker for the combination of pistachios and citrus, and for the high riffability factor of a good sponge cake recipe, so I sort of threw all those ideas into a blender (or stand mixer, as the case may be), and layered it with a dreamy pile of honeyed cream.

There are a few steps involved here, but it's actually better to make the cake and soak it in syrup the day before you fill and top it with the cream—making it perfect for a dinner party when you need to plan ahead. The cake gets even more irresistibly damp and flavorful with an overnight rest.

CAKE

6 large eggs, at room temperature

¾ cup (5⅜ ounces/150 grams) evaporated cane juice

1 teaspoon pure vanilla extract

1 teaspoon finely grated lime zest

1 teaspoon finely grated lemon zest

1 cup plus 2 tablespoons (5 ounces/ 142 grams) unbleached all-purpose flour, spooned and leveled

¾ cup (3¼ ounces/92 grams) shelled, roasted, unsalted pistachios*

½ teaspoon fine sea salt

¼ teaspoon baking powder

5 tablespoons (2½ ounces/71 grams) unsalted butter, melted and cooled slightly

1. Position a rack in the center of the oven and preheat the oven to 350°F. Butter an 8-inch, light-colored metal springform pan and line it with parchment paper or spray it with nonstick cooking spray.

2. Make the cake: Into the bowl of a stand mixer fitted with the whisk attachment, add the eggs, evaporated cane juice, vanilla extract, lime zest, and lemon zest. Beat on high speed until the mixture is very light and airy, quadrupled in volume, and the color of vanilla pudding, 7 to 8 minutes.

3. Into the bowl of a food processor fitted with the steel blade, combine the flour, pistachios, salt, and baking powder. Process until the nuts are very finely ground, about 1 minute.

*The best places to find the greenest roasted (and least expensive!) pistachios are Persian markets.

HONEY-CITRUS SYRUP

1 cup (8 ounces/226 grams) water

½ cup (6 ounces/168 grams) honey

2 tablespoons (1 ounce/28 grams)
freshly squeezed lime juice

1 tablespoon freshly squeezed
lemon juice

Pinch of fine sea salt

HONEY CREAM AND ASSEMBLY

4 ounces (113 grams) full-fat cream
cheese, at room temperature

2 tablespoons (1½ ounces/42
grams) honey

1 teaspoon pure vanilla extract

¾ cup (6⅜ ounces/180 grams)
heavy cream, chilled

¼ cup (1 ounce/30 grams) shelled,
roasted, unsalted pistachios,
coarsely chopped

4. Using a large flexible spatula, scoop out about a third of the pistachio flour and gently spoon it over the surface of the batter. Fold gently to blend. Repeat with the remaining two-thirds of the flour. Ensure the batter is well blended by gently tilting the bowl back and forth while you give the batter a few more folds, making sure there are no dry pockets in the mix or hiding at the bottom of the bowl.

5. Slowly, and in a thin stream, pour the melted butter over the surface of the batter in a large spiral (this will prevent the butter from immediately sinking to the bottom of the bowl). Gently fold the butter into the batter until thoroughly combined and no buttery streaks remain (don't worry if the batter loses a bit of volume while you fold in the butter).

6. Scrape the batter into the prepared pan and smooth the top. Bake until the cake is deeply golden, the surface springs back when lightly pressed, and a toothpick inserted into the center of the cake comes out clean, 45 to 50 minutes. Place the cake on a wire rack and allow the cake to cool slightly in the pan while you make the syrup.

7. Make the honey-citrus syrup: Into a medium saucepan, add the water, honey, lime juice, lemon juice, and salt. Stir gently over high heat as the syrup comes to a boil. Reduce the heat to medium-high and boil until the syrup has reduced to ¾ cup, 8 to 10 minutes.

8. Set the still-warm cake in the pan on a large plate. Using a wooden skewer, pierce the cake deeply all over, making holes about ½ inch apart in concentric circles. Very slowly pour about half of the hot syrup evenly over the

cake, giving it several seconds to absorb before you pour over the remainder. Let the cake rest for at least 3 hours (or up to overnight—the cake just gets better the longer it rests).

9. Make the honey cream: In the bowl of an electric mixer fitted with the whisk attachment, combine the cream cheese, honey, and vanilla extract. Beat on high speed until silky and aerated, about 2 minutes. Scrape the honeyed cream cheese into a medium bowl.

10. Pour the heavy cream into the mixer bowl (no need to clean the bowl first). Fit the whisk attachment back onto the mixer and whip the cream on high speed to stiff peaks.

11. Fold about one-fourth of the whipped cream into the cream cheese mixture. Scrape the cream cheese mixture into the bowl with the whipped cream and fold gently to blend well.

12. Assemble the cake: Carefully remove the soaked cake from the pan and transfer it to a cake plate. Use a long, serrated knife to slice the cake in half crosswise. Remove the top layer of the cake. Pile the honey cream onto the bottom layer, and smooth it evenly, leaving a ½-inch border around the edge of the cake.

13. Top the cake with the second layer, pressing it gently to adhere. Sprinkle the top of the cake with the chopped pistachios, patting them lightly as needed to encourage them to stick. Chill the cake uncovered for at least 30 minutes before slicing with a serrated knife and serving.

TIP: *If in doubt about the cake's doneness, err on the side of giving it a couple more minutes in the oven—even a slightly underdone sponge cake will just love to collapse on you. A soft, springy quality when pressed is your best indicator of it being fully baked.*

Honey: the sweet sophisticate

Weight: 1 tablespoon/¾ ounce/21 grams

Characteristics: Twice as sweet as sugar, ambrosial, earthy. Just like wine, honey can present an exciting wide variety of hues and flavor notes to pair with different ingredients, depending on the flowers from which the honeybees got their nectar.

Where it comes from: Bees! Lots and lots of hardworking bees. In fact, it takes about ten thousand bees, flying tens of thousands of miles and feeding on more than two million flowers, to make 1 pound of honey, which is only about 1⅓ cups (and you think you've got a busy schedule!). The average honeybee with a six-week lifespan only makes about one-tenth of a teaspoon of honey in its lifetime.

Bees use their long, tubelike tongues to suck the nectar from each flower, and they actually have two stomachs, with one specifically for holding nectar. When bees return to the hive, they transfer the nectar to worker bees that get down to the business of "chewing" it and transforming the complex sugars in the nectar to simple sugars. The nectar is then carried throughout the hive, where it can spread out and dry, aided by the worker bees fanning it with their wings. When the honey has thickened enough, it can be harvested. Honey is most often harvested in late summer or early fall.

Best uses: Softer baked goods that don't require crispness. Muffins and quick breads tend to be great for swapping in honey for white sugar, but keep an eye on the baking time because honey makes baked goods brown darker and faster. Homemade granola is a honeyed favorite of mine, as is using honey as a "seasoning" in recipes in conjunction with a more neutral sweetener like evaporated cane juice or brown rice syrup. I'm a big fan of using some honey in candies to really boost their flavor, like in the Orange Blossom Honey and Walnut Toffee on page 146, and the Honeycomb Candy on page 136. You can also look for granulated honey, which can be used like white sugar and has incredible flavor.

Bonus points: Because honey is much sweeter than sugar, you can use less of it in recipes and still get a sweet result. For the best nutritional punch, reach for raw honey, which is packed with B vitamins and vitamin C and has antibacterial, anti-inflammatory, and antioxidant properties. Many people swear by eating raw local honey to slowly build up a stronger tolerance for the pollens in their environments to relieve seasonal allergies.

How to store: Store in a tightly sealed container in a cool place away from direct sunlight. Honey doesn't need to be refrigerated, but it can sometimes become cloudy or crystallize when stored for a long period of time. If this happens, warm the honey briefly with gentle heat and it will become clear and fluid again.

Five-Flavors Party Cake

MAKES ONE 8-INCH 2-LAYER CAKE

Nothing brings out the dessert fangirl in me quite like the heavenly combination of honey, almonds, vanilla, lemon, and raspberries. If this quintet was a boy band, I'd be front and center, swooning all over the place.

A major bonus: Although I love any excuse to pull out my piping bag, I'm far from an accomplished cake decorator. So I love this cake because it basically decorates itself, with a layer of sugared almonds baked right into the top, and a few adorable raspberry "flowers" to add a little extra pretty to the whole thing.

PREPARING THE PANS

1 tablespoon unsalted butter, softened

½ cup (1¾ ounces/50 grams) sliced almonds

1 tablespoon plus 1 teaspoon evaporated cane juice

CAKE

1 cup (8 ounces/227 grams) whole milk, at room temperature

1 tablespoon freshly squeezed lemon juice

6 tablespoons (4½ ounces/126 grams) honey

½ cup (2½ ounces/72 grams) whole raw almonds*

2 cups (9 ounces/255 grams) unbleached all-purpose flour, spooned and leveled

1½ teaspoons baking powder

¾ teaspoon fine sea salt

½ teaspoon baking soda

1. Position the racks in the upper and lower thirds of the oven and preheat the oven to 350°F.

2. Prepare the cake pans: Generously grease the sides and bottoms of two 8-inch round cake pans with the butter. Sprinkle the bottoms of both pans with an even coating of almond slices. Dust evaporated cane juice over the almonds, about 2 teaspoons in each pan.

3. Make the cake: In a large measuring cup, whisk together the milk and lemon juice. Set aside for at least 10 minutes while you get the rest of your ingredients together (the milk will thicken and curdle—you're making homemade buttermilk!). Whisk in the honey.

4. In the bowl of a food processor fitted with the steel blade, process the almonds until very finely chopped, about 30 seconds. Add the flour, baking powder, salt, and baking soda. Blend for 1 full minute, or until the almonds have been ground to a powder.

*You can also use an equal weight of sliced almonds (or about ¾ cup) to grind up for the cake if you have extra.

13 tablespoons (6½ ounces/184 grams) unsalted butter, soft but still cool

1 cup (7 ounces/200 grams) evaporated cane juice

1 tablespoon finely grated lemon zest

1 tablespoon pure vanilla extract

½ teaspoon pure almond extract

5 large eggs, at room temperature

CREAM CHEESE FROSTING

4 ounces (113 grams) full-fat cream cheese, very soft and at room temperature

½ cup (1 stick/4 ounces/113 grams) unsalted butter, softened but still cool

2 tablespoons (1½ ounces/42 grams) honey

1 teaspoon pure vanilla extract

1 teaspoon freshly squeezed lemon juice

1 teaspoon finely grated lemon zest

½ cup (2 ounces/57 grams) organic confectioners' sugar, sifted

ASSEMBLY

12 ounces (340 grams) fresh raspberries

42 almond slices

5. In the bowl of a stand mixer fitted with the paddle attachment, beat together the butter, evaporated cane juice, lemon zest, vanilla extract, and almond extract on medium-high speed until light and fluffy, about 3 minutes. Add the eggs one at a time, giving each about 30 seconds to incorporate into the batter before adding the next.

6. Reduce the mixer speed to low. Alternately add the dry and wet ingredients in five additions, beginning and ending with the dry ingredients. Fold the batter by hand several times with a large flexible spatula to ensure the batter is well blended.

7. Divide the batter equally between the 2 prepared pans, smoothing the tops. Bake until the cakes are golden, a toothpick inserted in the center comes out clean, and the cakes spring back when lightly touched, 35 to 40 minutes. Cool the cakes completely in the pans. Run a thin knife around the edges of each pan and invert the cakes onto a work surface and examine them—they both should be gorgeously golden and almond-crusted. Choose the better-looking of the pair to be the top layer of the cake. Place the less fortunate cake layer almond side up on a cake plate (and tell her it's personality and flavor that really matter).

8. Make the frosting: In the bowl of an electric mixer, beat the cream cheese until totally lump-free. Add the butter and the honey and beat until smooth, scraping the bowl often with a flexible spatula. Beat in the vanilla extract, lemon juice, and lemon zest. Add the confectioners' sugar and mix until smooth.

9. Assemble the cake: Spoon the frosting into a piping bag fitted with a large round tip. Starting about ½ inch in from the very edge of the bottom cake layer, pipe a line of frosting around the entire cake, to create a sort of "frosting dam" and make for a nice clean appearance when the cake is stacked. Fill in the circle with frosting, and use the back of a spoon or a small spatula to smooth it out into an even layer, using the dam as your guide.

10. Place a row of raspberries in a circle, shoulder to shoulder, all around the outer edge of the frosting, checking the alignment occasionally, as this circle of berries will be visible once the cake is complete. Fill in the center with more berries. Pipe a few small dollops of frosting on top of the very center of the berries as "adhesive" for the top layer.

11. Top with the second cake layer, almond side up. Pipe 7 small clouds of frosting, evenly spaced, all around the perimeter of the cake. Top each little cloud with a fresh raspberry. Gently press 6 or 7 almond slices around each raspberry to form a flower. Chill the cake for about 30 minutes or until you're ready to serve, giving it 15 minutes or so to soften on the counter before slicing and serving.

Chocolate, Cherry, and Cacao Nib Pavlova

SERVES 6 TO 8

If I were forced to choose a favorite dessert and not allowed to say "all of them," my pick would be pavlova. Crisp meringue with a marshmallowy interior, pillows of cream, and a jumble of fruit—to me, it's an absolute symphony of textures and flavors, and a great way to play with seasonal fruits of all sorts. It's also one of the simplest and most impressive things to serve to the dinner party set. Oh, you're fancy now.

MERINGUE

1 batch of Crisp, Raw Sugar Meringue (see page 231, and see step 1 below), unbaked

2 tablespoons (⅜ ounce/12 grams) unsweetened natural cocoa powder

⅓ cup (2⅝ ounces/75 grams) cacao nibs

CHERRY TOPPING

12 ounces (340 grams) thawed frozen or fresh pitted dark sweet cherries

1 tablespoon turbinado sugar

1 teaspoon freshly squeezed lemon juice

1 teaspoon cornstarch

MASCARPONE CREAM

4 ounces (113 grams) mascarpone cheese at room temperature

1 teaspoon vanilla bean paste or pure vanilla extract

1 cup (8½ ounces/224 grams) heavy cream, chilled

¼ cup (1¾ ounces/50 grams) turbinado sugar

1. Position a rack in the center of the oven and preheat the oven to 225°F. Lay a sheet of parchment paper onto a baking sheet. Using a pencil, trace a 6½-inch circle onto the paper, and flip the paper over to line the baking sheet, so that the circle is still visible through the paper.

2. Begin to whip up a batch of Crisp, Raw Sugar Meringue. After you've added the vanilla, into a small bowl, sift together the cocoa from this recipe's meringue ingredients with the cornstarch from the meringue recipe. Gently

TIP: *For an even simpler version of this dessert, swap out the cooked cherry topping for a few handfuls of unsweetened, fresh seasonal berries.*

sift the cocoa mixture over the meringue and fold in carefully with a large flexible spatula. When just a few streaks of cocoa remain, fold in about two-thirds of the cacao nibs until well blended.

3. Pile the meringue onto the baking sheet at the center of the circle. Smooth the meringue onto the sheet, using the circle tracing as your guide (it will look a bit on the small side, but the meringue will spread as it bakes). Sprinkle the remaining cacao nibs over the meringue. Bake until dry and crisp on the surface, but with a bit of give underneath toward the center, about 2 hours. Turn the oven off and let the meringue cool completely in the oven, about 1 hour more.

4. Make the cherry topping: In a medium saucepan, combine the cherries, sugar, and lemon juice. Place the pan over medium heat and bring the mixture to a boil. Cook until the cherries release some of their juices, about 3 minutes. Keeping the heat on under the pan, remove 2 tablespoons of the juice to a small bowl. Whisk in the cornstarch until smooth. Pour the cornstarch mixture back into the pot and stir constantly for 1 minute, or until the liquid in the pot thickens slightly. Cool completely.

5. Make the mascarpone cream: In a medium bowl, use a handheld electric mixer on low speed to beat together the mascarpone cheese and vanilla bean paste or extract for about 30 seconds (don't overbeat, or the mixture will become grainy). In a separate medium bowl, use the handheld mixer to beat the cream and sugar to soft peaks, about 2 minutes. Gently fold the cream into the mascarpone mixture just until smooth.

6. To assemble the pavlova, place the meringue disk on a serving platter or cake stand. Pile about half the cream onto the meringue. Spoon on about half the cherry topping and a drizzle of sauce. Serve the remaining cream and cherries alongside the pavlova, slicing it like a pie.

TIP: *To make this even more dinner party–friendly, bake the meringue and prepare the topping up to 2 days ahead. Store the meringue in an airtight container and refrigerate the fruit, allowing it to come to room temperature before serving.*

A Tale of Two Meringues

Many pastry chefs will tell you that meringue cannot be made successfully without refined white sugar. Well! I've got news for you, fancy chef people. It can be done in the Real Sweet kitchen—you just have to get a little crafty, be specific about how you'll use the meringue, and above all, respect the sugar.

To start, there are three basic ways to make meringue: the French method, wherein egg whites are whipped with a gradual addition of sugar; the Swiss method, which involves whisking the whites with all the sugar at once in a heatproof bowl set over a pan of simmering water, so that the sugar can dissolve first before whipping; and the Italian method, where the sugar is heated to a syrup on the stove and then drizzled into whipping egg whites. In all cases, it's best to check the weather report: heat and humidity are the enemies of a lofty, stable meringue, so cool, dry days are your best bet for meringue making.

Crisp, Raw Sugar Meringue (see page 231 for recipe). To make this type of meringue for something like a base for a pavlova or crunchy cookies, you want a dry, granulated natural sugar. My sugar of choice is turbinado because it's so versatile, but you can also use piloncillo or muscovado sugars. The Swiss method is key here for crisp, dry baked meringue that holds its shape. While it might seem that the French method could work for this type of meringue, it's far from foolproof and typically yields tough, chewy, flat, or pockmarked meringues.

Soft, Fluffy Meringue (see page 234 for recipe). Ideal straight up as a marshmallow-type frosting or pie topping, for lemon meringue pie, or fortified with butter for a classic buttercream filling. We're not concerned about this type of meringue baking up crisp, so we can use liquid sugars here, like bold honeys and maple syrup. To make the sugars behave and create a stable egg white foam, though, they must first be heated as a syrup to 248°F, then be drizzled into whipping egg whites via the Italian method. This type of meringue can't be baked, because the liquid sweeteners will prevent the meringue from ever drying out (and even if they emerge from the oven dry at first, within moments of coming in contact with the air they'll soften and collapse), but it can be toasted with a kitchen torch or under the broiler for a brief moment. If soft, fluffy clouds of sweet heaven are the order of the day, this meringue is the way to go.

Praline Cream Roulade

SERVES 10

So pretty, so kitschy! You'd be hard-pressed to find a crowd that won't ooh and aah at this one. This tender, nutty cake is packed with the caramelized crunch of pralines.

CAKE

¾ cup (3⅜ ounces/96 grams) unbleached all-purpose flour, spooned and leveled

⅓ cup (1½ ounces/43 grams) chopped pecans, ground fine in a food processor

1 teaspoon baking powder

½ teaspoon fine sea salt

¼ cup (2 ounces/57 grams) whole milk

1 teaspoon pure vanilla extract

5 large eggs, separated, plus 1 large egg white, at room temperature

¾ cup (5¼ ounces/150 grams) turbinado sugar

PRALINE CREAM

¾ cup (5¼ ounces/148 grams) turbinado sugar

2 tablespoons (1 ounce/28 grams) water

1 teaspoon agave nectar or honey

¼ teaspoon fine sea salt

½ teaspoon pure vanilla extract

⅔ cup (2⅝ ounces/75 grams) chopped pecans

1½ cups (12¾ ounces/360 grams) heavy cream, chilled

Homemade Confectioners' Sugar (see page 193) or organic confectioners' sugar, for serving

1. Position a rack in the center of the oven and preheat the oven to 350°F. Butter a 12 × 17-inch baking sheet or spray it with nonstick cooking spray. Line the bottom of the pan with a sheet of parchment paper and grease the paper, too.

2. Make the cake: In a medium bowl, whisk together the flour, ground pecans, baking powder, and salt.

3. In a small heatproof bowl, heat the milk in the microwave on high power for 1 minute (or in a small saucepan on the stove over medium heat, being careful to not let it boil). Stir in the vanilla extract.

4. In the bowl of an electric mixer fitted with the whisk attachment, beat the egg whites on medium-high speed until soft peaks form, 2 to 3 minutes. Gradually add ¼ cup of the turbinado sugar. Beat until the whites hold very stiff, glossy peaks, about 2 minutes more. Transfer the whites to a clean bowl and set aside.

5. In the bowl of the electric mixer (no need to clean it first), combine the egg yolks with the remaining ½ cup of turbinado sugar. If using a stand mixer, switch to the paddle attachment. Beat the yolks on high speed until very thick, light in color, and triple in volume, 6 to 7 minutes. Reduce the mixer speed to low and stir in the milk mixture. Gradually stir in the flour mixture. When just a few streaks of flour remain, stir the batter gently by hand until well blended.

6. Fold one-third of the egg whites into the yolk mixture, to lighten the batter. Gently fold in the remaining whites. Pour the batter into the prepared pan and smooth the top with an offset spatula. Bake for 15 minutes or until the cake springs back when lightly touched (rotate the cake 180 degrees halfway through the baking time).

7. Smooth a clean tea towel out onto a large work surface and cover it with a sheet of parchment paper. Invert the cake onto the parchment. Peel back the parchment from the cake. With the shorter side closest to you, carefully roll up the warm cake away from you. Transfer it to a wire rack to cool completely.

8. Make the praline cream: Spray a baking sheet with nonstick cooking spray or line it with a silicone baking mat. Combine the turbinado sugar, water, agave nectar, and salt in a small saucepan. Place the pan over high heat and stir gently with a heatproof spatula. When the mixture begins to boil, stop stirring. Cook the syrup until it begins to caramelize, swirling the pan occasionally.

9. After several minutes, the syrup will take on a deep amber hue, and the edges of the large bubbles on the surface of the syrup will be darker than their interiors. As soon as you see the edges of the bubbles turning darker and smell a smoky caramel fragrance coming from the syrup, remove the pan from the heat. Immediately stir in the vanilla extract and the chopped pecans (the sugar will begin to crystallize a bit as you stir and that's okay!). Turn the praline mixture out onto the prepared baking sheet and smooth it into as even a layer as possible. Cool completely.

10. Break the cooled praline into chunks and place them into the bowl of a food processor. Process until finely ground (but be careful not to process too long, or you'll get nut butter).

11. To assemble the cake, in a medium bowl whip the cream to stiff peaks. Fold the ground praline into the cream.

12. Slowly unroll the cooled cake. Spread the filling evenly over the cake, leaving about a 1-inch border on all sides. Reroll the cake, leaving the parchment paper behind. Gently slide both hands under the rolled cake and quickly transfer it to a serving platter. Chill for at least 1 hour before serving, or up to 6 hours ahead. Dust with confectioners' sugar before slicing.

Toblerone Tart

MAKES ONE 9-INCH TART

Inspired by the iconic candy bar, this tart is intense on all levels—it's a looker but also full of flavor. And thanks to a pile of fluffy, toasted honey meringue to mimic those honey-almond nougat bits in the chocolate bar, it's also on the sweet side, so one little sliver really goes a long way.

8 ounces (227 grams) bittersweet chocolate (70% to 72% cacao), finely chopped

2 ounces (57 grams) unsweetened chocolate, finely chopped*

1 cup plus 2 tablespoons (9½ ounces/270 grams) heavy cream

2 tablespoons (1½ ounces/42 grams) honey

⅛ teaspoon fine sea salt

½ teaspoon pure vanilla extract

¼ teaspoon pure almond extract

⅔ cup (2½ ounces/70 grams) coarsely chopped almonds, toasted and cooled

One 9-inch Nutty Graham Crust (see page 240), baked and cooled

1 batch of Soft, Fluffy Meringue (see page 234), made with honey

SPECIAL EQUIPMENT

A small kitchen torch**

1. Make the filling: Place both chopped chocolates in a large heatproof bowl. In a small saucepan, combine the cream, honey, and salt. Set the pan over high heat. Bring the cream just to a simmer, stirring to dissolve the honey. Remove the pan from the heat. Stir in the vanilla and almond extracts. Pour the hot honeyed cream over the chocolate, and let stand for 5 minutes. Whisk the ganache until smooth and shiny. Fold in the almonds. Pour the ganache into the crust. Chill the tart until the ganache is very firm, about 2 hours, or up to one day ahead.

2. Pile the meringue onto the center of the tart, using the back of a spoon to create fluffy, fanciful swirls. With a kitchen torch, toast the meringue to your liking. Chill until ready to serve, up to 4 hours in advance.

* This tiny amount of unsweetened chocolate is essential to balance the intense ambrosial sweetness of the honey. I go a bit higher on the cacao percentage for the bittersweet chocolate, too, to make sure the filling really has an edge.

** Really the best tool for the job here. But to use a broiler, spread the meringue all the way to the edges of the tart to protect the ganache from the heat, and broil for 60 seconds.

Strawberry and Lemon Cream Puffs

MAKES ABOUT 1 DOZEN 2½-INCH PUFFS

I can think of many, many things to say about cream puffs, but "ethereal decadence" is one of the first terms to come to mind. Once you get the hang of making pâte à choux pastry, you'll become a cream-puff-and-éclair-and-profiterole-making machine, stuffing them with every dreamy combination you can think of. Here a dollop of honey-sweetened lemon curd is transformed into a mousselike filling and sandwiched with gleaming berries.

PUFF DOUGH

½ cup (4 ounces/113 grams) nonfat milk*

4 tablespoons (2 ounces/57 grams) unsalted butter, cut into small pieces

1 tablespoon turbinado sugar

¼ teaspoon fine sea salt

½ cup (2¼ ounces/64 grams) unbleached all-purpose flour, spooned and leveled and sifted

2 large eggs, at room temperature

½ teaspoon pure vanilla extract

FINISHING THE PUFFS

1 large egg

1 tablespoon water

Pinch of fine sea salt

Turbinado sugar, for sprinkling

*Typically, whole milk is recommended for baking because it adds richness and moisture, but for pâte à choux I prefer nonfat or skim milk, which yields a crisper puff. If you only have low-fat (2%) or whole milk, use a mixture of half water, half milk.

1. Make the puff dough: Position an oven rack in the center of the oven and preheat the oven to 400°F. Line a baking sheet with parchment paper.

2. In a small heavy-bottomed saucepan (about 1½ quarts), combine the milk, butter, sugar, and salt. Place the pan over medium-high heat and bring the mixture to a simmer, stirring occasionally to encourage the butter to melt. Bring the mixture to a boil. Add the flour all at once, lower the heat to medium, and immediately begin stirring at a good clip with a wooden spoon—don't let up until the dough starts to come off the sides of the pan in a loose ball and a light crust forms on the bottom of the pan, about 2 minutes.

3. Turn the dough into the bowl of a standing mixer fitted with the paddle attachment. On medium speed, mix the dough to cool it a bit, about 30 seconds. When the steam subsides, beat in 1 egg until completely incorporated. Beat in the vanilla extract and then add the second egg. Continue mixing on medium speed for 1 full minute, or until the dough is smooth but sticky and elastic in appearance. Test the dough's readiness by grabbing a pinch of dough between your thumb and forefinger,

LEMON CREAM AND ASSEMBLY

⅔ cup (5⅝ ounces/160 grams)
heavy whipping cream, chilled

⅓ cup (2⅞ ounces/82 grams)
Honey-Vanilla Lemon Curd
(see page 226)

1½ cups (8⅞ ounces/250 grams)
sliced fresh strawberries

1 teaspoon honey

TIP: *Swap out the lemon juice for lime juice in the curd for a refreshing flavor pairing with strawberries.*

TIP: *Skip the puffs altogether and pile the lemon cream and berries onto a disk of Crisp, Raw Sugar Meringue (see page 231) for a killer pavlova.*

rubbing them together, and pulling them apart—the dough is ready when you can pull your fingers apart and stretch a string of dough between them about 1 inch in length.

4. Drop 12 rounded portions of dough, each about 2 tablespoons, 2 inches apart onto the prepared baking sheet.

5. Finish the puffs: In a small bowl, beat together the egg, water, and salt until well blended. Brush each puff with the egg wash, and follow with a generous sprinkling of sugar.

6. Bake the puffs for 15 minutes at 400°F. Rotate the baking sheet from front to back and reduce the temperature to 375°F. Continue baking until the puffs are deeply golden and sound hollow when their exteriors are tapped, 10 to 15 minutes more. Crack the door of the oven, turn it off, and let the puffs cool for 5 minutes in the oven. Carefully transfer the puffs to a wire rack to cool completely.

7. Make the lemon cream: In a medium bowl, whip the cream to stiff peaks. Gently fold the lemon curd into the whipped cream until well blended.

8. Toss the strawberries with the honey.

9. To assemble, slice the puffs in half crosswise. Place the bottoms of the puffs on 6 dessert plates. Dollop 2 generous tablespoons of lemon cream onto each puff. Divide the strawberries equally among the puffs. Sandwich the cream and berries with the tops of the puffs, pressing down gently to adhere.

Homemade Confectioners' Sugar

Whether you call it "powdered sugar" or "confectioners' sugar," this gloriously snowy, sweet powder is an essential in a baker's pantry. The confectioners' sugar you find in the supermarket is made from refined white sugar and a starch to prevent clumping, typically cornstarch. Nothing adds a bit of pretty to a simple cake or cookie (or hides a sunken middle or slightly overdone crust) quite like it, and it's also a great addition to doughs and batters that turn out delicate, slightly crumbly finished products, like shortbread.

I'm a fan of organic confectioners' sugar, which is made from less refined (and vegan) evaporated cane juice and cornstarch and/or tapioca starch. But whether organic or not, the sugar and starch are ground until powdery, and voilà—you end up with confectioners' sugar.

But even organic store-bought confectioners' sugar is on the more refined end of the sugar scale, and sometimes it's nice to have something a little more natural for recipes that call for confectioners' sugar (and without an extra trip to the store). In that case—make your own! Here's what you need:

1 cup (7 ounces/200 grams) turbinado sugar, rapadura, or coconut sugar

+

1 tablespoon cornstarch or tapioca starch

+

1 full minute in a clean coffee grinder or high-powered blender

=   Homemade Confectioners' Sugar

Use immediately, or store in an airtight container in a cool, dry place. Granted, when you use this homemade confectioners' sugar made with richly hued sweeteners in place of refined supermarket powdered sugar, you won't get a snow-white pile of frosting, but you will be rewarded with phenomenal flavor and the satisfaction of MacGyvering your way to a less refined version of a store-bought ingredient.

Spoonable Sweets

I CAN'T THINK of too many things that make me feel more accomplished and totally domesticated than making my own ice creams and custards. No matter what exotic sugars you toss into the mix, there's just something so fantastically old-fashioned about deciding to take the time to churn or whisk up something yourself that could so easily be store-bought. It's always so surprising how simple and crave-worthy these kinds of icebox desserts are—the ingredient lists are short, the hands-on time is marginal, and all you have to do is chain yourself to something heavy to keep from opening the fridge or freezer every 20 minutes to poke at them with a spoon as they chill.

Butterscotch Pôts de Crème

SERVES 8

Once upon a time, in our early married lives, my husband and I lived in a tiny apartment near the beach in Los Angeles. Right about the time we moved up north to San Francisco, the restaurant scene in that area of L.A. really started to explode. One of those spots, Gjelina in Venice, has drawn in celebrities and gorgeously groomed food lovers ever since. Gjelina's entire menu is worth braving the long wait for a table, but the butterscotch pôt de crème is legendary. The first time I had it, I immediately started trying to replicate it. I'll never have movie stars sashaying through my kitchen, but I can have my pôt de crème and eat it, too—two at a time while wearing sweatpants and no makeup. Now *that's* living.

6 large egg yolks

4 tablespoons (2 ounces/57 grams) unsalted butter

½ cup (4 ounces/113 grams) firmly packed light or dark muscovado sugar

½ teaspoon fine sea salt

2¼ cups (19⅛ ounces/540 grams) half-and-half

¾ teaspoon vanilla bean paste or pure vanilla extract

Whipped cream, for serving

Buttermilk Caramel Sauce (see page 225), for serving

Flaky sea salt (such as Maldon), for serving

1. Position a rack in the center of the oven and preheat the oven to 325°F. Set 8 small (6- to 8-ounce) ramekins, cups, or coffee cups in a small roasting pan. Bring a kettle of water to a boil.

2. In a medium bowl, whisk the egg yolks until smooth.

3. In a medium saucepan over medium heat, melt together the butter, sugar, and salt. Whisking often, cook until the sugar begins to caramelize, darkening in color and smelling nutty, 3 to 4 minutes. Carefully and slowly whisk in the half-and-half. The caramel will seize at first, melting back into the mixture once all the liquid is added. Stirring often, bring the mixture to a simmer. Remove the pan from the heat. Stir in the vanilla bean paste or vanilla extract.

4. Whisk a small amount of the hot liquid into the yolks to warm them and then gradually whisk in the remainder. Set a fine mesh sieve over a large heatproof measuring cup. Pour the custard through the sieve. Divide the custard evenly among the ramekins.

5. Slide out the oven rack and place the roasting pan on the rack. Carefully fill the roasting pan with boiling water halfway up the ramekins, taking care not to splash any water into the custards. Slide the rack back into place. Bake until the custards are just set but still jiggle when tapped and a thin knife inserted into the center of one of the custards comes out clean, 30 to 45 minutes, depending on the size, depth, and thickness of the ramekins (use the "jiggle test" and knife tester as your clues for doneness). Let the custards cool out of the roasting pan for 5 minutes. Cover loosely with plastic wrap and chill for 3 to 4 hours.

6. To serve, top each pôt de crème with a dollop of whipped cream, a drizzle of caramel sauce, and a smattering of flaky sea salt.

TIP: *These pôts de crème are so dense, so creamy, so full of sweet-salty butterscotch flavor that a 4-ounce portion is all anyone really wants or needs. Even putting it in tiny 2-ounce ramekins would be plenty. This stuff is serious.*

Agave Nectar: the girl next door

Weight: 1 tablespoon/¾ ounce/21 grams

Characteristics: Super-sweet (more than twice as sweet as white sugar), versatile, mild in flavor with no bitter aftertaste (darker varieties are a touch stronger in flavor).

Where it comes from: The best agave nectars come from the blue agave plant, which can be found in the volcanic soils of southern Mexico. The plant itself resembles the top of a giant pineapple, with long, thick leaves. Once the plant reaches maturity at about 7 to 10 years old, the leaves are harvested and their sap—called *aguamiel*, or "honey water"—is extracted. The sap is then filtered and heated, ideally at no more than 118°F to retain the nutrients, to create a thicker syrup. (The sap can also be fermented to make tequila, but that's another book.)

Best uses: In candies to prevent crystallization; in fruit desserts where its relatively neutral flavor can allow other flavors to really shine; in frozen desserts such as ice creams and sorbets, where it lends softness and scoopability, as in the ice creams on pages 206 and 214; and when you need to convert a recipe with honey to be vegan, agave nectar makes a good, easy substitution. With a thinner consistency than honey, agave nectar is great for sweetening all kinds of drinks and cocktails.

Bonus points: Anti-inflammatory and antibacterial properties (the Aztecs used agave sap right from the plant to treat wounds). It's also a low glycemic sweetener. Teaspoon for teaspoon, agave nectar has more calories than white sugar, but because it has more than twice the sweetness, you can use less agave and still achieve a sweet result.

Additional buzz: As a sweetener, agave nectar isn't without controversy—although it is low on the glycemic index, it's also very high in fructose, which many experts recommend avoiding in large quantities. Additionally, some brands are subjected to extreme processing and high heat, which destroys any of agave's benefits. To get the best product possible and retain some nutrients, I always look for raw, organic blue agave from trusted sources. Because it's so light in flavor, I also tend to use it in recipes as more of a backup sweetener in conjunction with another sugar rather than making agave the main event.

How to store: Store in a sealed container in a cool, dark place.

Caramelized Honey and Sea Salt Gelato

MAKES 1 GENEROUS QUART

Attention: If you're the couch-it-with-a-pint-of-ice-cream kind of person, I have two things to say: First, call me. Second, this ambrosial, sweet-and-salty combination is otherworldly, giving the whole salted caramel trend a run for its money. Honey is cooked to the point of caramelization, rendering it bold and sweet and nutty, and with a generous smattering of sea salt, you've got lazy evening sweet tooth satisfaction of the highest order. Bonus points for experimenting with bolder and exotic flavored honeys, as they'll really shine in this recipe.

2¾ cups (22 ounces/627 grams) whole milk

1 tablespoon cornstarch

1 cup (8½ ounces/240 grams) heavy cream

½ vanilla bean, split lengthwise*

½ teaspoon flaky sea salt (such as Maldon), plus an extra ¼ teaspoon at the end (optional)**

½ cup plus 1 tablespoon (6⅝ ounces/189 grams) honey

1 tablespoon water

1 teaspoon freshly squeezed lemon juice

1. In a small bowl, whisk together ½ cup of the milk and the cornstarch until dissolved. Set aside.

2. In a large (4-quart) saucepan, combine the remaining 2¼ cups milk, the cream, and the vanilla bean (it may look as if the pan is much too big, but you'll need the room once the hot honey is added later). Set the pan over medium heat and bring the mixture to a bare simmer—don't let it boil. Remove the pan from the heat.

3. In a medium saucepan, gently stir together the honey, water, and lemon juice. Cook over medium-high heat, swirling the pan occasionally, until the honey is deeper in color and has a nutty fragrance, about 5 minutes. The

*I especially love a Tahitian vanilla bean here; its floral notes get along beautifully with honey.

**Using just ½ teaspoon of flaky sea salt makes for a lovely balanced gelato with the barest hint of saltiness. If you're a true salty-sweet fanatic like me, add in the additional ¼ teaspoon and experience more pronounced little sparks of salt within the waves of sweetness as you eat the gelato.

longer you let the honey cook, the more pronounced the caramelized flavor will be, but don't let it burn—your nose will lead the way. Remove the pan from the heat. Standing back, carefully drizzle the honey into the milk, just a tablespoon or so at a time, whisking all the while to keep the mixture from bubbling up too violently. When all the honey has been added, put the pan back on the heat. Bring the gelato back up to a low boil over medium heat.

4. When the gelato is just beginning to bubble, whisk in the milk and cornstarch. Continue whisking for 1 minute, or until the mixture thickens and provides some resistance as you stir. Remove the pan from the heat. Pour the gelato into a heatproof bowl (I like a metal bowl for faster cooling). Set in the refrigerator to chill until completely cold, at least 4 hours or overnight.

5. Pour the gelato into an ice cream maker and churn according to the manufacturer's instructions. If desired, for an extra salty-sweet punch, stir in ¼ teaspoon of flaky sea salt right before packing the gelato into an airtight container. Freeze until firm, at least 2 hours.

TIP: *Depending on the honey you use, you might get so much foam bubbling on the surface that it can be difficult to gauge how dark the honey is getting; in that case, dip a light-colored wooden spoon or heatproof spatula in the pot from time to time to check the color.*

Grown-Up Chocolate Pudding

MAKES ABOUT 3 CUPS

During both of my pregnancies, I had an insatiable urge for pudding. And not some hifalutin pudding, either. Let's just say that the more plastic packaging that was involved with said pudding, the more satisfied I was with it. These days, I'm back to making stovetop puddings from scratch (that pregnancy "free pass" only lasts so long, unfortunately). Whether with child or not, it's hard to resist a bowl of spoonable comfort, but often scratch puddings can be a little lackluster in the flavor department. That's definitely not the case here.

Enter barley malt syrup, a kind of obscure sweetener with a very unique, complex flavor that can be a tough sell in recipes. It's not a malt flavor that hits you over the head like a milkshake made with the powdered stuff; this is really more about the genuine mellow earthiness of real malt and its ability to round out the sharp, bittersweet edge of good cocoa powder and chocolate. I also love the silkiness that a liquid sweetener like this can lend to creamy desserts. Add some smoky dark muscovado sugar to the mix, and you've got the biggest, baddest chocolate pudding in town.

⅓ cup (4 ounces/113 grams) barley malt syrup

¼ cup (2 ounces/57 grams) firmly packed dark muscovado sugar

3 large egg yolks

2 tablespoons (½ ounce/16 grams) cornstarch

1 tablespoon unsweetened natural cocoa powder

¼ teaspoon fine sea salt

1¾ cups (14 ounces/397 grams) whole milk

2 ounces (57 grams) bittersweet chocolate (60% to 70% cacao), chopped

1 tablespoon unsalted butter

2 teaspoons pure vanilla extract

1. In a medium heavy-bottomed saucepan, whisk together the malt syrup, sugar, egg yolks, cornstarch, cocoa powder, and salt (you may have a few small lumps of sugar in the mix). Set the pan over medium-high heat. Slowly whisk in the milk. When the mixture is warm to the touch, stir in the chocolate until melted. Reduce the heat to medium and continue whisking occasionally until the pudding has thickened considerably, about 8 minutes. Do not let the pudding come to a simmer while you wait for it to thicken—if it appears that it's threatening to bubble, pull the pan from the heat for a brief moment, then return it, whisking all the while.

2. When the pudding has thickened, whisk in the butter and vanilla extract until smooth. Pour the pudding into a heatproof container and cover the surface with plastic wrap, being sure to get the wrap directly in contact with the surface of the pudding to avoid a skin (if you're a pudding skin lover, ignore this step). Chill completely in the refrigerator, at least 3 hours.

TIP: *If you accidentally overcook the pudding and it begins to curdle a bit, don't fret! Simply scrape the pudding into a blender or food processor and blitz until silky smooth.*

Vegan Chocolate-Almond Sorbet

MAKES 1 GENEROUS QUART

Like a frozen ganache; a cloak of creamy chocolaty goodness, studded with crunchy salted almonds, and yet . . . vegan? Pinch me.

2¼ cups (18 ounces/510 grams) unsweetened almond milk

2 teaspoons cornstarch

¾ cup (6 ounces/170 grams) firmly packed dark muscovado sugar

⅔ cup (2⅓ ounces/67 grams) unsweetened natural cocoa powder

1 tablespoon light agave nectar

½ teaspoon fine sea salt, plus extra for salting the almonds

4 ounces (113 grams) dairy-free bittersweet chocolate (60% to 70% cacao), finely chopped*

1 teaspoon pure vanilla extract

⅔ cup (2⅝ ounces/75 grams) raw almonds, chopped

*Be sure to read the label to confirm that your chocolate is dairy-free to make this treat vegan.

1. In a small bowl, combine ¼ cup of the almond milk with the cornstarch. Whisk to dissolve.

2. In a large (4-quart) saucepan, whisk together the remaining 2 cups of almond milk, sugar, cocoa powder, agave nectar, and salt. Place the pan over medium-high heat and bring the mixture to a low boil. Boil for 1 minute. Whisk in the cornstarch mixture. Continue whisking for 1 minute more, until thickened. Remove the pan from the heat and add the chopped chocolate and vanilla extract. Whisk until smooth.

3. Set a fine-mesh sieve over a medium heatproof bowl. Pour the sorbet base through the sieve. Cover the bowl with aluminum foil and refrigerate until completely chilled, at least 4 hours. Whisk vigorously to smooth out any lumps. Pour into an ice cream maker and churn according to the manufacturer's instructions.

4. Toast the almonds: Place a dry, medium skillet over medium-high heat. Add the almonds and sauté until pale golden in spots and fragrant, 6 to 7 minutes. Sprinkle with fine sea salt. Cool completely.

5. When the sorbet is finished churning, fold in the cooled almonds. Pack into an airtight container and freeze until firm. Let soften for about 15 minutes before serving.

Vegan Toasted Coconut Chip Ice Cream

MAKES 1 GENEROUS QUART

Next to cilantro, politics, and going to carnivals, coconut has got to be one of the most polarizing things on the planet. But if you're a coconut lover (and I raise my fist with you!), this combination of creamy coconut milk and toasty, nutty shards of tropical goodness is just the ticket. Oh! And a little chocolate. Because unlike carnivals and me, coconut and chocolate just belong together.

2 14-ounce cans (28 ounces/794 grams) full-fat coconut milk

2 tablespoons (½ ounce/16 grams) cornstarch

6 tablespoons (4½ ounces/126 grams) light agave nectar

¼ teaspoon fine sea salt

½ vanilla bean, split lengthwise

1 cup (2⅞ ounces/80 grams) unsweetened shredded coconut

⅓ cup (2 ounces/57 grams) dairy-free bittersweet chocolate (60% to 70% cacao), finely chopped

1. Start by giving the cans of coconut milk a good shake to homogenize the milk as much as possible before using it. In a small bowl, combine ½ cup of the coconut milk and the cornstarch and whisk to dissolve.

2. Pour the remaining coconut milk into a large (4-quart) saucepan. Whisk in the agave nectar and salt and drop in the vanilla bean. Set the pan over medium-high heat and bring the mixture to a low boil. Whisk in the cornstarch mixture. Continue to whisk for 1 full minute, or until the mixture is noticeably thicker, resembling a thin pudding. Remove the pan from the heat. Pull the vanilla pod out and scrape any remaining seeds into the pot, whisking to blend.

3. Set a fine-mesh sieve over a medium heatproof bowl. Pour the ice cream base through the sieve into the bowl. Cover the bowl with aluminum foil and refrigerate until the mixture is completely chilled, at least 4 hours. Whisk the ice cream base to smooth out any lumps. Pour the mixture into an ice cream maker and churn according to the manufacturer's instructions.

4. While the ice cream is freezing, toast the coconut: Preheat the oven to 350°F. Spread the coconut in an even layer on a clean, dry rimmed baking sheet. Bake until golden, 6 to 7 minutes, stirring often and keeping a close eye on the coconut—it can go from perfectly golden to burned in a matter of seconds! Pour the toasted coconut onto a plate to cool.

5. When the ice cream is finished churning, fold in the cooled, toasted coconut and chocolate bits. Pack into an airtight container and freeze until firm. Let the ice cream soften on the counter for about 15 minutes before serving.

Raspberry Lemonade Yogurt Pops

MAKES ABOUT TEN 2½-OUNCE POPSICLES

These creamy pops are like a smoothie on a stick. The spark of lemon, tart yogurt, and hit of vanilla give these gems a bit of an edge over your standard fruity, icy treats.

12 ounces (340 grams) fresh or thawed frozen raspberries

⅔ cup (8 ounces/224 grams) light agave nectar or honey

½ cup plus 3 tablespoons (5½ ounces/156 grams) water, divided

1 vanilla bean, split lengthwise

1 tablespoon freshly squeezed lemon juice

1 teaspoon finely grated lemon zest

⅛ teaspoon fine sea salt

1 cup (8½ ounces/240 grams) 2% Greek yogurt

1. In a medium saucepan, combine the raspberries, agave nectar, ½ cup water, vanilla bean, lemon juice, lemon zest, and salt. Set the pan over medium-high heat and stir gently until the mixture comes to a full boil. Remove the pan from the heat and let cool completely. Pull the vanilla pod from the pan. Using the back of a knife, scrape any remaining vanilla seeds into the pan, and discard the pod.

2. Pour the raspberry mixture into a blender or the bowl of a food processor fitted with the steel blade. Puree until smooth. Add the yogurt and remaining water and process until well blended. Transfer the mixture to a large spouted measuring cup for easy pouring, and pour into Popsicle molds. Insert wooden sticks. Freeze until firm.

Mango Lassi Frozen Yogurt

MAKES 1 GENEROUS QUART

Packed with Indian-inspired flavors, this ice cream recipe utilizes the simplest method in history—no cooking on the stovetop, and everything just gets thrown into the food processor. It also uses jaggery, a classic Indian sweetener that tastes like a buttery, light brown sugar. So heaven, basically.

Jaggery, like piloncillo, comes caked in large cubes that must be grated on the large holes of a box grater before measuring and adding it to recipes. After it's grated, just pack it lightly into the measuring cup, as you would for regular brown sugar. And use a serrated knife to chop some into a generous handful of small hunks and shards while you're at it—folded into the ice cream, they make for crunchy, sugary nubbins that blow toffee bits out of the water.

One 16-ounce (454-gram) bag frozen mango chunks (about 3 cups), partially thawed

1½ cups (12¾ ounces/360 grams) half-and-half or heavy cream✱

¾ cup (4 ounces/113 grams) grated jaggery

½ cup (4¼ ounces/120 grams) 2% Greek yogurt

2 tablespoons (1 ounce/28 grams) freshly squeezed lime juice

¾ teaspoon ground cardamom

½ teaspoon finely grated lime zest

⅛ teaspoon fine sea salt

¼ cup (1⅜ ounces/38 grams) finely chopped jaggery

✱ Use one or the other, or a combination of both, depending on the richness you prefer.

In the bowl of a food processor fitted with the steel blade, combine the mango, half-and-half, grated jaggery, yogurt, lime juice, cardamom, lime zest, and salt. Process until mostly smooth with just a few small chunks of mango in the mix. Scrape into your ice cream maker and freeze according to the manufacturer's instructions. Fold in the chopped jaggery. Transfer to a 6-cup container, cover tightly, and freeze until firm.

TIP: *If you can't find jaggery, grated panela or piloncillo (its Latin American counterparts) works just fine.*

Espresso, Rapadura, and Bittersweet Chocolate Semifreddo

SERVES 8 TO 10

If you're an American child of the eighties, you might remember those super-fancy-pants commercials for an ice cream dessert called Viennetta. I still remember begging for it "in our grocers' freezer section," and the taste sensation—ripples of cool, milky, aerated ice cream, with whisper-thin layers of crisp chocolate throughout that gently snapped between the teeth—still lingers in my file from the one time my wish was granted. I hear that Viennetta can still be found in other, luckier places on the planet. But in my adult life, I have to try and relive my Viennetta dreams with semifreddo.

Semifreddo means "half-cold" in Italian, but to me it means all the pleasure of homemade ice cream, without having to haul out the ice cream maker. It's somehow light and unbelievably rich at the same time, and it melts on the tongue like a sweet, creamy cloud. Earthy rapadura gives the sweetness here an edge, and its nutty brown color begs to be paired with espresso and crisp shards of bittersweet chocolate.

2½ ounces (71 grams) bittersweet chocolate (60% to 70% cacao), melted

3 large eggs, separated*

3 large egg whites

¼ teaspoon fine sea salt

⅔ cup (4 ounces/113 grams) rapadura

8 ounces (224 grams) mascarpone cheese, at room temperature

¾ teaspoon pure vanilla extract

¾ teaspoon instant espresso powder**

1. Line a baking sheet with parchment paper or a silicone baking mat. Line a 9 × 5 × 3-inch loaf pan with 2 perpendicular sheets of plastic wrap, leaving at least 3 inches of overhang on all sides.

2. Spread the chocolate in a very thin layer onto the prepared baking sheet in a rough 8 × 12-inch rectangle. Set the sheet pan in the refrigerator or freezer to set the chocolate.

3. Into the bowl of a standing mixer fitted with the whisk attachment, pour the egg whites. Add the salt. Begin

*Use pasteurized eggs if you're concerned about consuming raw eggs.

**If you can't find instant espresso powder (I like Medaglia d'Oro brand), use 1½ teaspoons instant coffee crystals.

TIP: *This is great all on its own, but to dress up the dessert plates a bit, Homemade Chocolate Syrup (page 230) makes for a nice little sauce on the side.*

beating the whites on medium-high speed, just until they reach soft peaks. Add ⅓ cup of the rapadura, a small spoonful at a time, allowing each addition to incorporate into the egg whites for several seconds before adding more. After the rapadura has been added, continue beating until the egg whites are stiff and glossy. Scrape the egg whites into a clean bowl and set aside.

4. Pour the egg yolks and remaining ⅓ cup of rapadura into the mixer bowl (no need to clean the bowl first). Whip on high speed until the mixture is paler in color and very thick, about 5 minutes. Add the mascarpone cheese, vanilla extract, and espresso powder. Beat again on high speed until the mixture is thickened and smooth, about 1 minute. Remove the bowl from the mixer and fold the mixture several times by hand to be sure everything is evenly incorporated. Fold about a quarter of the egg whites into the yolk mixture to lighten it. Gently fold in the remaining meringue until no streaks of egg white remain.

5. Remove the sheet pan with the chocolate from the refrigerator or freezer. Gently break the chocolate sheet into irregular shards (if your hands tend to be a bit warm, fold up the sides of the parchment or baking mat to serve as a barrier between your hands and the chocolate as you break it, to keep from melting it).

6. Fold the chocolate shards into the semifreddo mixture. Scrape into the prepared pan and smooth the top. Pull the plastic wrap overhang over the semifreddo, making sure it's completely covered. Freeze at least 8 hours, or overnight.

7. To serve, unwrap the semifreddo, invert it onto a serving platter, and remove the plastic wrap. Slice into thick slabs.

Rhubarb and Rose Ice Cream

MAKES 1 GENEROUS QUART

A long time ago, at the very beginning of the macaron craze, I sampled a raspberry and rose confection that was so overpoweringly rose-flavored it was like munching on a Valentine's Day bouquet. Blech. It had me swearing off floral-infused sweets for years to come.

When adding flowery flavorings to sweets, it's easy to go overboard. I use only small amounts of delicate flower waters instead of stronger oils and have since changed my tune about floral notes in desserts. Adding a touch of rose or orange blossom water to something isn't actually about giving it a "flowery" taste—ideally, you don't even know the flower water is there; you'd only notice it if it wasn't. It's really about enhancing other ingredients, particularly fruits. Here the rose water just heightens the springlike tang of the rhubarb, making the ice cream simply taste beautifully "pink."

3 cups trimmed, chopped rhubarb, from about ¾ pound (340 grams) rhubarb stalks✱

¾ cup plus 1 tablespoon (9⅝ ounces/273 grams) light agave nectar or honey

2 tablespoons (1 ounce/28 grams) water

1 teaspoon freshly squeezed lemon juice

2 cups (17 ounces/482 grams) heavy cream

2 cups (16 ounces/454 grams) whole milk

1 vanilla bean, split lengthwise

4 large egg yolks

⅛ teaspoon fine sea salt

2 tablespoons (1 ounce/28 grams) rose water

1. Begin by making the rhubarb puree. In a medium saucepan, stir together the rhubarb, ¼ cup of the agave nectar, the water, and the lemon juice. Set the pan over high heat and bring to a boil. Reduce the heat to low, and simmer, stirring occasionally, until the rhubarb is so soft it falls apart and transforms into a pool of bright pink threads, about 10 minutes. Transfer the entire contents of the pan to the bowl of a food processor or blender. Puree until smooth. Scoop out 1¼ cups puree to a large bowl—if there's excess puree, store it in the refrigerator for another use (delicious stirred into yogurt!).

✱ Look for the darkest, reddest rhubarb that you can find to end up with a barely blush pink ice cream. If you like, you can bump up the color with a few drops of natural red food coloring (see page 115) or genuine grenadine.

2. To make the ice cream base, pour the cream and milk into a medium saucepan and add the vanilla bean. Bring to a bare simmer over medium heat—do not boil. Cover the pan and let steep for 10 minutes. Pull out the vanilla bean and scrape any remaining vanilla seeds into the pot.

3. In another large bowl, whisk together the egg yolks, the remaining agave nectar, and salt. Slowly stream the hot cream into the yolks, whisking all the while. Pour the custard back into the saucepan. Set the pan over medium heat. Stirring often, scraping the sides and bottom of the pan as you go, cook the custard until it is thickened and coats the back of a spoon (if you run your finger through the coating on the spoon, a track should remain). Whisk the custard into the rhubarb puree. Whisk in the rose water. Cover tightly with plastic wrap and refrigerate until thoroughly chilled, at least 3 hours.

4. Pour the custard into an ice cream maker and freeze according to the manufacturer's instructions. Transfer the soft ice cream to a lidded container and freeze until firm.

STRAWBERRY, RHUBARB, AND ROSE ICE CREAM

Stir 1 cup (6 ounces/170 grams) diced fresh strawberries into the churned ice cream before its final freeze.

Custard in Two Directions

SERVES 6

This custard fits two of my favorite culinary criteria: simple and endlessly riffable. It's a formula that can be sweetened with a number of different natural sugars and can be made in two ways—sugar side up, as in a crème brûlée, or sugar side down, served as a flan—a glorious little number that makes its own caramel sauce as it bakes. When inverted, the sweet sauce cascades over the top and onto the plate in a gleaming golden pool.

The base recipe here can be made with a number of different dry sugars just to sweeten the custard—light or dark muscovado, demerara or turbinado, maple sugar, coconut sugar, all work here. I especially love playing with the sugar in the custard base, because with such simple ingredients accompanying it (just eggs, milk, and a bit of cream), you can really taste the flavor nuances of the different sugars. And you get to enjoy the sugar in two different ways, both in the custard and on it, either as a crunchy crust or as a luscious sauce.

Of course, it makes sense to use the same sugar to sweeten the custard as you do for either the brûlée topping or the sauce. What I found, though, is that some sugars are better than others, depending on the direction in which you'll be serving the custard. Grated piloncillo is my top pick for a versatile sugar that can take this custard in either direction. But for a crème brûlée, where the sugar will be torched before serving, my favorite is demerara or turbinado sugar—coconut sugar and moist muscovado sugars tend to burn before they can develop a nice caramelized cap on the custard. When you're making a flan, though, light muscovado and coconut sugars are the best, with their bold flavors and beautiful deep golden brown colors.

¾ cup (4 ounces/113 grams) grated piloncillo

1½ cups (12 ounces/340 grams) whole milk

½ cup (4¼ ounces/120 grams) heavy cream

½ vanilla bean, split lengthwise

4 large egg yolks

1 large whole egg

¼ teaspoon fine sea salt

1. Position a rack in the center of the oven and preheat the oven to 325°F. Set six 8-ounce ramekins into a metal baking pan or small roasting pan. To serve the custard flan-style, smooth 1 tablespoon of the sugar into an even layer across the bottom of each ramekin. To serve the custard as crème brûlée, set aside 6 tablespoons of the sugar in a small bowl.

2. In a small saucepan, combine the milk, cream, and vanilla bean. Set the pan over medium-high heat. Heat the milk until it's hot to the touch and steaming but not yet simmering. Cover the pan and let steep for 5 minutes. Bring a kettle of water to a boil.

3. In a large bowl, whisk together the egg yolks, egg, and remaining 6 tablespoons of sugar for 1 continuous minute, until the mixture is noticeably lighter in color and slightly thickened.

4. Remove the vanilla pod from the saucepan, and scrape any remaining seeds into the milk, discarding the pod. Whisk about 2 tablespoons of the hot milk into the egg mixture. Add another 2 tablespoons, whisking to blend. Pour the remaining milk into the bowl in a steady stream, whisking all the while, until the custard is well blended. Pour the custard through a fine mesh sieve set over a large measuring cup (the spout of the cup makes it easy to pour the custard into the ramekins).

5. Divide the mixture equally among the 6 ramekins. Open the oven and slide out the center rack. Set the baking pan on the rack. Pour the boiling water into the baking pan until the water level rises about halfway up the sides of the ramekins, being careful not to splash any water into the custards. Slide the rack carefully back into the oven. Bake the custards until they are just set, still jiggling quite a bit, but a knife comes out clean, about 30 minutes. Let the custards cool out of the roasting pan for 5 minutes. Cover loosely with plastic wrap and chill for 3 to 4 hours.

6. To serve the custards flan-style, run a thin knife around the edge of the ramekins and invert the custards onto dessert plates. For crème brûlée, smooth 1 tablespoon of the reserved sugar over the top of each custard. Use a kitchen torch to melt and brown the sugar until bubbling and crisp. Allow to set for 5 minutes before serving.

Maple Cloud Pudding

SERVES 6

This creamy, spoonable dessert is a bit like panna cotta meeting a maple cloud. I love eating this straight up, scattered with toasted nuts for a bit of crunch; you can also use it to make a killer Maple Cream, Chocolate, and Walnut Tart (see page 172).

2½ teaspoons (¼ ounce/7 grams) unflavored powdered gelatin✱

¼ cup (2 ounces/57 grams) cold water

¾ cup (6⅜ ounces/180 grams) heavy cream, chilled

3 large egg yolks, at room temperature

7 tablespoons (5⅛ ounces/ 147 grams) pure maple syrup (dark or very dark preferred)

¼ teaspoon fine sea salt

½ teaspoon vanilla bean paste or pure vanilla extract

½ cup (2 ounces/57 grams) chopped walnuts or pecans, toasted and salted (see page 79)

✱ For gelatin sheets, use 8 grams gold-strength sheets (finding the correct strength sheets and weighing them is the key to successful converting). Soak them in cold water until soft, wring them out, and proceed with the rest of the recipe.

TIP: *The pudding can also be frozen in individual ramekins, piped into ice pop molds, or smoothed into a square metal baking pan and scooped out for a mousselike ice cream.*

1. In a small bowl, whisk together the gelatin and water. Set aside to soften for at least 5 minutes.

2. In the bowl of an electric mixer fitted with the whisk attachment, whip the cream to firm peaks. Transfer the whipped cream to a medium bowl. Clean the mixer bowl and pour in the egg yolks. Fit the mixer with the paddle attachment. Beat the egg yolks on high speed until lightened in color and texture, about 5 minutes.

3. In a small saucepan, combine the maple syrup and salt. Set the pan over high heat and bring the syrup to a boil. Boil for 30 seconds and then remove the pan from the heat. Stir in the vanilla bean paste or extract. Scrape the softened gelatin into the syrup and whisk until the gelatin has melted completely.

4. Return the mixer speed to medium. Slowly drizzle the hot syrup into the yolks. Raise the speed to medium-high and beat until the custard has begun to thicken to the consistency of honey and the bowl is cool to the touch, about 5 minutes—beating too long will cause the gelatin to set.

5. Using a flexible spatula, fold in about a third of the whipped cream into the yolk mixture. Add the remaining whipped cream and fold gently to blend. Divide the pudding among 6-to 8-ounce ramekins. Garnish with a smattering of toasted nuts.

Melon, Honey, and Mint Granita

SERVES 6

Every once in a while—say, in the peak of summer when temperatures are ghastly and you've invited people over for dinner when you'd really rather just lie in front of the air conditioner in your underpants—life calls for something light, fruity, and totally refreshing. Granita is my go-to for these occasions, and it couldn't be simpler.

The honey in this recipe offers a twofer—not only does its ambrosial sweetness play beautifully with fragrant melon and fresh mint, it also keeps the puree from freezing solid, making it easier to scrape the granita into a gorgeous, fluffy pile of sweet snow.

1 cup (1½ ounces/42 grams) tightly packed fresh mint leaves

½ cup (4 ounces/113 grams) water

⅓ cup (4 ounces/113 grams) honey

1 tablespoon freshly squeezed lime juice

⅛ teaspoon fine sea salt

1 large very ripe cantaloupe, about 4 pounds (1.8 kilograms), peeled and cut into 1-inch chunks

1 tablespoon very finely chopped fresh mint, for garnish (optional)

TIP: *Frozen dessert glasses make for a gorgeously frosty presentation and help keep the granita cold while eating it: simply run the glasses under cold water and place them in the freezer for several minutes prior to portioning out the granita.*

1. In a medium saucepan, combine the mint leaves, water, honey, lime juice, and salt. Set the pan over high heat and bring the mixture to a boil, stirring all the while to encourage the leaves to wilt. Remove the pan from the heat and cover it. Let cool and steep for 30 minutes. Strain the syrup into a clean bowl, pressing on the mint leaves in the strainer to extract as much mint flavor as possible. Discard the mint leaves.

2. Place the melon chunks in a blender or the bowl of a food processor fitted with the steel blade. Puree until nearly smooth. Pour in the mint syrup and blend until the mixture is as smooth as possible. Slosh the puree into a 9 × 13-inch baking dish. Place the dish in the freezer until the surface and edges of the puree have begun to freeze, about 45 minutes (it will still be somewhat liquid underneath). Use the tines of a fork to gently loosen the ice crystals from the edges of the pan, and scrape the icy surface. Freeze for another 30 minutes, and scrape the granita again, breaking up any large chunks and fluffing

them as you scrape and stir. Repeat the freezing and scraping process until the entire pan is a frozen, fluffy bed of icy, fruity crystals.

3. To serve, scoop generous spoonfuls of granita into frozen dessert glasses. For an extra punch of mint, stir a handful of finely chopped mint leaves into the finished granita before spooning it into the serving glasses.

Frostings, Fillings, and Accoutrements

WHEN IT COMES TO SWEET TREAT MAKING, sometimes it's not about making one type of cookie or showstopper cake that can stand on its own. Sometimes you need a little building block recipe that you can riff on and mix and match with other elements to create a dish that truly is your own. Or maybe you just need a little dollop, dab, or drizzle of something exciting that can jazz up the everyday. The recipes in this chapter are the ones to have in your toolbox for when you're really feeling inspired to play with natural sugars in the kitchen.

TIP: *You can serve this sauce slightly warm or straight from the fridge—it thickens a touch when chilled, but it is still very pourable.*

Buttermilk Caramel Sauce

MAKES ABOUT 1⅓ CUPS

When I first started developing this recipe, I was thinking about how buttermilk might help to trim the fat a bit on what is typically a really rich sauce. But awesomely, you get so much more than that when buttermilk is introduced into the mix—the tang helps to offset the sweetness, and when added into a salted caramel like this one, along with the toasty notes of turbinado or piloncillo? Whoa, mama.

 This sauce is not like your traditional caramel sauce at all—it's something else altogether. Ice cream should be so lucky. (It's also smack-the-table good on pancakes and waffles, if you really like your breakfast partner.)

1 cup (7 ounces/200 grams) turbinado sugar or grated piloncillo

2 tablespoons (1 ounce/28 grams) water

1 tablespoon honey, brown rice syrup, or agave nectar*****

½ teaspoon fine sea salt

4 tablespoons (2 ounces/57 grams) unsalted butter, cut into cubes

½ cup (4¼ ounces/120 grams) well-shaken buttermilk

½ cup (4¼ ounces/120 grams) heavy cream

¼ teaspoon pure vanilla extract

* Any of these liquid sweeteners will work to keep the caramel from crystallizing. Honey tends to come forward in this sauce and adds a nice flavor note. Brown rice syrup and agave are more utilitarian here, with agave being sweeter than brown rice syrup.

1. In a medium heavy-bottomed saucepan, gently stir together the sugar, water, honey, and salt. Set the pan over medium-high heat. Stirring gently, bring the mixture to a boil, and then stop stirring. Cook the sugar syrup until it caramelizes, about 5 to 7 minutes, swirling the pan occasionally. The color of the sugar will make it a bit tough to gauge by sight if the sugar is caramelizing, so watch for a thickening of the syrup and a few wisps of smoke coming from the pot, and keep your nose tuned in for a slightly smoky smell; if you'd like to use a candy thermometer for extra insurance, caramelization will happen at about 300°F.

2. Remove the caramel from the heat and whisk in the butter. Carefully whisk in the buttermilk and cream. Place the pan back on the heat and bring the caramel back up to a simmer, whisking all the while. Cook for 1 additional minute; if any lumps formed when you poured in the liquids, they should smooth out completely during this time. Remove the pan from the heat again and whisk in the vanilla extract. Chill in the refrigerator until you're ready to serve.

Honey-Vanilla Lemon Curd

MAKES 1 GENEROUS CUP

Lemon curd is the sort of thing that's so easy to make and tastes so incredible, you wonder why you're not making it all the time. And when you use honey instead of sugar and add fresh vanilla bean, it takes the whole thing to another ambrosial level. If Meyer lemons are in season, I hoard them—they make for the very best lemon curd of all.

Although the gelatin in this recipe isn't necessary, it gives the lemon curd a firmer set. Since I like to use it for things like layering cakes and folding into whipped cream (as in the Strawberry and Lemon Cream Puffs on page 190), I add the gelatin to make an all-purpose curd. But if you'll just be using it as a spread or topping, the gelatin can be omitted in step 1 (just add the full ⅓ cup lemon juice to the saucepan in step 2).

⅓ cup (2⅝ ounces/75 grams) freshly squeezed lemon juice (from about 2 medium lemons)

½ teaspoon unflavored powdered gelatin

3 large egg yolks

1 whole large egg

½ cup (6 ounces/168 grams) light-colored, mild-tasting honey*

1 tablespoon finely grated lemon zest

⅛ teaspoon fine sea salt

½ vanilla bean, split lengthwise

2 tablespoons (2 ounces/57 grams) unsalted butter, cut into small cubes and chilled

TIP: *This recipe doubles well, and when packed into pretty half-pint jars, makes great gifts. For gifting, pour the curd from the blender into sterilized jars and cap tightly. Store in the refrigerator for up to 3 weeks.*

1. In a small bowl, whisk together 1 tablespoon of the lemon juice and the gelatin. Let soften for 5 to 10 minutes.

2. In a small to medium saucepan, whisk together the egg yolks, egg, honey, remaining lemon juice, lemon zest, and salt. Submerge the vanilla bean in the pan. Place the pan over medium heat. Whisk constantly, occasionally scraping the bottom of the pan, until the curd is thickened and threatens to begin bubbling. It will also coat the back of a spoon, and if you run your finger through the curd across the back of the spoon, a track will remain. Remove the vanilla bean and discard it. Add the lump of softened gelatin and whisk until melted. Whisk in the butter, one piece at a time, until smooth.

3. Pour the curd through a sieve, using a flexible spatula to coax it through, into a heatproof bowl. Cover the surface with plastic wrap. Chill until thickened, about 3 hours.

*The lighter-colored the honey, the better to avoid an unappealing brownish cast to the finished curd; light agave nectar works well here, too.

Caramelized Coconut Sugar Frosting

MAKES ABOUT 1½ CUPS

Not only is the flavor of this frosting positively dreamy, the transformation of it from something that looks like an ice cream topping to whipped caramelized clouds is pretty dang magical. You'll want to slather this on anything that's not nailed down.

9 tablespoons (4½ ounces/128 grams) unsalted butter, cut into tablespoons and softened

3 tablespoons (2¼ ounces/63 grams) brown rice syrup or light agave nectar*

¼ teaspoon fine sea salt

¾ cup (4 ounces/113 grams) coconut sugar

¼ cup (2 ounces/57 grams) heavy cream

1½ teaspoons pure vanilla extract

*Although the liquid sweetener here obviously adds sweetness, its main functions are to keep the caramel flexible and add a beautiful gloss to the whipped frosting. I like to use something very neutral in flavor, such as brown rice syrup, to allow the coconut sugar flavor to really shine, but you could also use light agave, mild honey, or even coconut nectar, if you have it, which will give a much deeper color to the frosting and make it a bit sweeter as well.

TIP: *Keep a close eye on the thermometer, and pull the pan from the heat the moment the temperature hits 248°F—coconut sugar can burn quickly and take on a somewhat astringent taste.*

1. In a medium heavy-bottomed saucepan set over medium heat, melt together 4 tablespoons of the butter, the brown rice syrup, and salt. Add the coconut sugar and stir with a heatproof spatula. Bring to a gentle boil and clip a candy thermometer onto the pan. Cook to 248°F, about 5 minutes. Remove the pan from the heat and carefully stir in the cream and vanilla extract. Cool for 10 to 15 minutes.

2. Whisk the remaining 5 tablespoons of butter into the caramel, a tablespoon at a time, letting each knob of butter absorb into the caramel before adding the next. Don't rush this step—you're not only setting yourself up for a nice emulsified frosting, you're also slowly cooling the caramel, both of which will make for a smooth, creamy final product.

3. Scrape the caramel into a mixing bowl or bowl of a stand mixer. Chill until the caramel is cool to the touch all the way through, about 20 minutes. Using an electric mixer fitted with the whisk attachment or a handheld mixer on medium speed, whip the caramel into a lush, creamy frosting until light and fluffy, about 2 minutes. (If it still looks like caramel sauce after 1 minute of beating, chill further before whipping again.) Use immediately, or store in a tightly covered container in the refrigerator for up to 1 week, bringing it back to room temperature before giving it a quick rewhipping.

HOMEMADE SWEETENED CONDENSED MILK

Full disclosure: Despite having lived my adult life in California, I am a midwestern gal at heart. And I'm sorry, Fancy Food Police, but my childhood in Illinois was full of gloriously kitschy desserts, heavy on plenty of less-than-natural ingredients. I still hold some of these recipes dear (hello, Mom's perfect cheesecake made with Bisquick), and during both of my pregnancies, cravings for crazy desserts that hadn't touched my lips in decades were suddenly pulled from my sensory files. Let's just say that both of my second trimesters found me with frozen tubs of nondairy whipped topping on the supermarket conveyor belt. True story.

Now, I can't honestly say that the present-day reality of some of these treats was always as awesome as I remembered (I'm looking at you, cake-from-a-box mix, soaked in Day-Glo Jell-O, frosted in that aforementioned Cool Whip), but there are a few gems from my gramma's recipe box that can definitely hang with the most hipster artisan desserts that seem to be everywhere these days. And more often than not, I find that many of these old-school recipes can be easily tweaked to cut down on some of the unpronounceable ingredients and make them even more spectacular.

As any lover of kinda-trashy dessert recipes will tell you, canned sweetened condensed milk is clutch. It's also a little creepy. I mean, gooey milk? In a can? That can outlive us all? Hmmm. There's got to be a better way. And guess what? There is! This homemade version works just as well in recipes that call for sweetened condensed milk, with whatever unrefined sugar will best match the recipe you're making, and even organic dairy, if you so desire. And dang, is it ever tasty.

1½ cups (12 ounces/340 grams) whole milk

⅔ cup (4¾ ounces/134 grams) evaporated cane juice or granulated natural sugar of your choosing

2 tablespoons (1 ounce/28 grams) unsalted butter

½ teaspoon pure vanilla extract

In a medium heavy-bottomed saucepan set over medium heat, combine the milk and sugar. Bring to a simmer, stirring often to dissolve the sugar. When the sugar is dissolved, reduce the heat to its lowest setting. Simmer until the liquid is reduced by half, stirring often (a heatproof flexible spatula is great for occasionally scraping the bottom of the pot to make sure nothing clings and burns). Stir in the butter and vanilla extract. Cool completely before storing in an airtight container in the refrigerator for up to 1 week or before using in recipes.

Homemade Chocolate Syrup

MAKES ABOUT 1¼ CUPS

Sometimes when children are really exceptionally adorable, they should be treated to an extra-large, frosty glass of chocolate milk, with as much chocolate syrup as they want. This version is sweetened with maple, to take the edge off of what will inevitably be a beverage made of equal parts milk and chocolate syrup. (It's excellent in coffee drinks and over ice cream, too.)

½ cup (6 ounces/168 grams) pure maple syrup

½ cup (1⅝ ounces/48 grams) unsweetened natural cocoa powder

½ cup (4 ounces/113 grams) water

⅛ teaspoon fine sea salt

½ teaspoon pure vanilla extract

In a small saucepan, combine the maple syrup, cocoa powder, water, and salt. Whisk to blend. Place the pot over medium-high heat, and as the mixture warms, continue whisking until the cocoa has dissolved and the syrup is smooth. Bring to a boil, and let the syrup reduce until slightly thickened, whisking occasionally, about 3 minutes. Whisk in the vanilla extract. Let the syrup cool before pouring into a storage container with a tight-fitting lid or into a squeeze bottle. Store in the refrigerator for up to 1 month.

Crisp, Raw Sugar Meringue

MAKES ABOUT 5 DOZEN 1½-INCH COOKIES, OR AN 8- OR 9-INCH PAVLOVA

Even in its most basic state with just a breath of vanilla added, this meringue made with turbinado is infinitely more flavorful than when it's made with white sugar. Of course, you can also dress up this building block recipe with any extracts that you like. See page 185 for more on this meringue method.

1 cup (7 ounces/200 grams) turbinado sugar

4 large egg whites

½ teaspoon cream of tartar

¼ teaspoon fine sea salt

1 teaspoon pure vanilla extract

1 tablespoon plus 2 teaspoons (½ ounce/14 grams) cornstarch

TIP: *When "baking" a meringue, what you're really doing is drying it out. It can be difficult for some ovens to maintain a temperature as low as 250°F or less, but don't sweat it. I recommend keeping an oven thermometer in your oven and checking it from time to time. As long as the temperature hangs out around 250°F or under, you're good.*

1. Position a rack in the center of the oven and preheat the oven to 250°F. Line a baking sheet with parchment paper or a silicone baking mat.

2. In the heatproof bowl of an electric mixer, combine the sugar, egg whites, cream of tartar, and salt. Bring a saucepan of water to a simmer over medium-low heat. Set the mixing bowl over the pan and whisk until the mixture is thick and hot to the touch with no sugar granules (test it by pinching the liquid between your fingertips and rubbing them together; make sure no sugar has sunk to the bottom of the bowl).

3. Fit the bowl onto a stand mixer fitted with the whisk attachment. Beat on high speed until the meringue is stiff, glossy, and voluminous, and the sides of the bowl are cool to the touch, 8 to 10 minutes. Beat in the vanilla extract. Using a large, flexible spatula, gently fold in the cornstarch to blend well.

4. For meringue cookies, drop the meringue by tablespoonfuls onto the baking sheet. Bake until completely dry on the surface and hollow-sounding when tapped lightly, about 1½ hours. Turn the oven off and let the meringues cool completely in the oven, about 1 hour more.

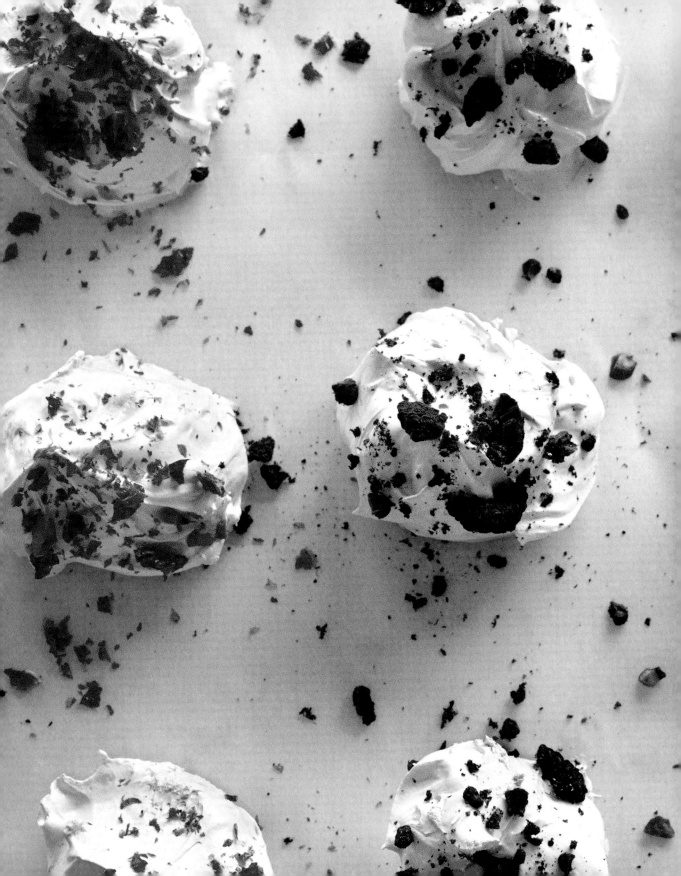

5. To turn the meringue into a base for a pavlova, smooth the meringue batter onto the prepared baking sheet into a 6½-inch circle. Bake for about 2 hours, or until crisp on the outside with a bit of give under the surface toward the middle, indicating a gloriously marshmallowy center. (See page 182 for a recipe using this technique.)

TIP: *After spooning or piping meringue cookies, you can jazz them up with any dry, brittle topping that won't keep the meringues from drying out—my favorites are finely chopped nuts and lightly crushed colorful freeze-dried fruits such as mandarin oranges and raspberries (Mother Nature's sprinkles!).*

Soft, Fluffy Meringue

MAKES ABOUT 5 CUPS

Honeyed (or mapled!) clouds of sweet, creamy (yet miraculously nonfat) fluff, perfect for frosting and piping onto cakes and cupcakes, and topping pies and tarts. Dreamy, right? Although the method here is like making an Italian meringue, using honey instead of white sugar creates a soft meringue that doesn't bake well (see page 231 for a meringue that bakes up crisp). Used straight up in its softly whipped state, however, this is the stuff of dessert-topping dreams.

3 large egg whites, at room temperature

2 teaspoons cornstarch

⅔ cup (8 ounces/224 grams) honey or pure maple syrup

2 tablespoons (1 ounce/28 grams) water

¼ teaspoon fine sea salt

2 teaspoons pure vanilla extract

TIP: *While you drizzle the syrup into the whipping egg whites, aim for the space between the whisk and the bowl rather than pouring it directly over the meringue. Letting the syrup run down the curve of the bowl a bit will keep it from spinning all over the sides of the bowl.*

1. Into the bowl of an electric mixer fitted with the whisk attachment, add the egg whites. Whip on medium-high speed until soft peaks form. Add the cornstarch and continue whipping until the whites reach firm peaks, about 1 minute more. Stop the mixer.

2. In a medium saucepan, combine the honey, water, and salt. Set the pan over high heat. Stir the mixture gently to combine as it heats to a boil. When the syrup has begun to bubble, clip a candy thermometer onto the side of the pan. Cook the syrup until the temperature reaches 248°F. Remove the pan from the heat, and with a mitted hand, carefully carry it over to the mixer. Restart the mixer on medium speed. Slowly drizzle the syrup into the whipping egg whites—just a tablespoon or two at first to avoid scrambling the whites. When all the syrup has been added, increase the mixer speed to high and whip the meringue until it is stiff and glossy, and the bowl is cool to the touch, about 5 minutes. Beat in the vanilla extract during the last minute of beating.

3. Use immediately as a frosting or filling.

My Favorite Vanilla Bean Buttercream

MAKES ENOUGH TO GENEROUSLY FROST 2 DOZEN CUPCAKES OR ONE 8- OR 9-INCH 2-LAYER CAKE

Sometimes life hands us a celebration (or an especially long workweek) that cries out for a cake involving copious amounts of butter and sugar and throwing all nutritional common sense out the window. For those moments, nothing hits the spot quite like a cake smeared with swirls of a simply made fluffy American buttercream.

Although not really a "buttercream" by the fancy pastry definition, an American-style confectioners' sugar–based frosting is pure indulgence for a sweet tooth (thanks to several parts more sugar than butter), and it is dead simple. My favorite version, though, flips the script on the standard ratio for American buttercream. It's not as sweet, and light as air. Using organic confectioners' sugar made with evaporated cane juice and tapioca starch is a just a touch less refined (though not by much, admittedly) and is especially great in this type of frosting—I find it has an even better mouthfeel in the finished product than standard-issue powdered sugar.

3 cups (12 ounces/340 grams) organic confectioners' sugar, sifted twice

3 tablespoons (1½ ounces/42 grams milk, half-and-half, or heavy cream

1 teaspoon vanilla bean paste or 2 teaspoons pure vanilla extract✶

⅛ teaspoon fine sea salt

1½ cups (3 sticks/12 ounces/340 grams) unsalted butter, at cool room temperature✶✶

✶ Vanilla bean paste is my favorite ingredient for flavoring frostings, both for its bold flavor and beautiful vanilla seed flecks. You can use 2 teaspoons pure vanilla extract instead.

✶✶ I love to use luxurious European-style butter (such as Plugrá) for this frosting to make it extra special.

Place the confectioners' sugar in the bowl of an electric mixer fitted with the paddle attachment. Add the milk, vanilla bean paste, and salt. On low speed, mix until the confectioners' sugar is evenly moistened (it will still look quite dry). Add the butter pieces and gradually increase the speed from low to medium-high. Beat until fluffy and lightened in texture, with a whipped appearance, 3 to 4 minutes. Adjust the texture of the frosting as needed with just an extra teaspoon of milk or cream at a time.

TIP: *This frosting cries out to be jazzed up with food coloring—see page 115 for the lowdown on more natural alternatives to using artificial colors.*

TIP: *For a sturdy frosting, be sure the butter is softened but still cool to the touch. A waxy look is good; shiny butter means it's too warm and will make a sloppy frosting.*

Maple and Vanilla-Roasted Fruit

MAKES 3 TO 4 CUPS, DEPENDING ON THE FRUIT VARIETIES

This idea of slowly roasting fruit with maple sugar, vanilla bean, and a hit of citrus is really more of a method than a true recipe. I use a number of different seasonal fruits here—in winter, it's 2 each of apples, pears, and Fuyu persimmons; in fall, it can be apples, grapes, and figs; and in spring and summer, nothing brings you closer to heaven than roasted peak-of-season peaches and nectarines, spooned over vanilla ice cream.

⅓ cup (2⅛ ounces/61 grams) maple sugar

1 vanilla bean

1 teaspoon finely grated lemon zest

2 pounds (908 grams) seasonal fruit, peeled, halved, cored and/or pitted

1 tablespoon freshly squeezed lemon juice

1 tablespoon unsalted butter, cut into small bits

2 tablespoons (1 ounce/28 grams) water

1. Position a rack in the center of the oven and preheat the oven to 375°F.

2. Place the sugar in a small bowl. With a sharp knife, split the vanilla bean in half lengthwise and scrape the seeds into the sugar (reserve the vanilla pod). Work the sugar, vanilla seeds, and lemon zest together with your fingertips until the sugar is fragrant and moist-looking.

3. Arrange the fruit in a 9 × 13-inch metal baking dish, cut side up. Drizzle with the lemon juice and sprinkle on the sugar. Dot the butter bits all over the fruit. Add the vanilla pod and water to the dish.

4. Roast for 30 minutes, spooning the pan juices over the fruit occasionally. Turn the fruit and continue to roast, basting once or twice, until tender, 15 to 20 minutes more.

5. Serve straight up or with a bit of ice cream, yogurt, or crème fraîche.

Maple: the gentle giant

Weight: 1 tablespoon/¾ ounce/21 grams

Characteristics: Twice as sweet as white granulated sugar, pure maple syrup has a gentler sweetness when compared with other liquid sweeteners such as honey or agave nectar; earthy, rich, round flavor. Comes in various grades that range from mild flavored to surprisingly bold.

Where it comes from: Most of the world's pure maple syrup comes from the boiled sap of sugar maple trees (and some red, black, or silver maples, too), found mainly in Canada and the northern United States, where Vermont is the top producer. For more than thirty years, maple syrup sold in the United States was labeled either Grade A (with light, medium, and dark amber varieties) or Grade B. Grade C was also sold commercially, for candy and baked goods. In Canada, where Quebec produces three-quarters of the world's maple syrup supply, there were three grades—#1, #2, and #3. These grades were always indicative of the color and depth of maple flavor of the syrup, not its quality or how refined or nutrient-rich it was, but there was concern that consumers might think otherwise.

So in 2014, the International Maple Syrup Institute slowly began rolling out a new, descriptive labeling system to be applied worldwide, doing away with "grades" completely. In 2015, shoppers will find that all maple syrup is labeled according to its depth of color and flavor: Golden Color/Delicate Taste; Amber/Rich Taste; Dark/Robust Taste; and Very Dark/Strong Taste (which will stand in as the Maple Syrup Formerly Known as Grade B, or #3 in Canada).

The season for collecting maple sap is called maple sugaring season, and it hits between early February and April. When a tree is mature enough (between thirty and forty years old), a hole is drilled into the trunk and a spout or tube is "tapped" into place to allow the sap to drip out. Sap collection usually lasts for 4 to 6 weeks. The sap is then boiled, filtered, and bottled. The later in the season the trees are tapped, the darker and bolder in flavor the finished syrup will be. The sap can also be dried to make maple sugar.

Best uses: Beyond the breakfast table, maple syrup is a superstar in a baker's pantry. Muffins, quick breads, and cakes (like the Maple Chocolate Cake on page 101), puddings and custards, and some candies all work well with maple syrup. Fruit-forward recipes, like those with pumpkin, apples, pears, berries, and stone fruits can benefit from a hit of maple. Bittersweet chocolate and maple make a dynamite flavor pairing, too.

Different types of pure maple syrup can be used interchangeably in recipes—an easy way to pump up the color and maple flavor of a dish. For recipes that call for white sugar, try ¾ cup maple sugar for every cup of white sugar—its bold flavor allows you to use a bit less sugar overall. Maple sugar is a spendy but oh-so-worth-it ingredient—I save it for recipes where it can really shine, like Maple Sugar Butter Cookies (page 90), or candies like Maple Marshmallows and Maple Spun Sugar (pages 140 and 157, respectively).

Bonus points: Awesome flavor aside, pure maple products are mineral powerhouses. They contain manganese, which is key for energy production, riboflavin for metabolic support, and immunity-boosting zinc in addition to calcium, potassium, and iron. Maple syrup is also low in fructose, making it the top sweetener choice of many nutritional experts.

How to store: Maple syrup doesn't have enough sugar in it to act as a natural preservative. Because of this, it's best to keep pure maple syrup tightly sealed and refrigerated after opening to prevent spoiling (and prolong your investment, as pure maple syrup isn't cheap!). Pure maple sugar, on the other hand, should be kept in an airtight container in a cool, dry place to prevent clumping.

Nutty Graham Crust

MAKES ONE 9-INCH CRUST

This nutty, crisp, sweet-salty graham crust is super versatile—use any nut that complements the filling you're using. These amounts yield a shallow crust perfect for tarts or the bottom of a cheesecake. To make enough crust for a deeper pie plate, make 1½ times the recipe.

Baking and cooling the crust makes it delightfully crisp and lends a textural element to filled pies and tarts, but you can skip the baking altogether and just chill the crust in the fridge to set it—about 30 minutes will do the trick.

⅓ cup (1¾ ounces/50 grams) raw almonds, walnuts, pistachios, or other nuts

5 ounces (140 grams) Homemade Graham Crackers (about 18 2½-inch crackers; see page 48) or 9 store-bought graham rectangles, such as Mi-Del brand

¼ teaspoon fine sea salt

3 tablespoons (1½ ounces/43 grams) unsalted butter, cut into small pieces

1½ tablespoons (1 ounce/28 grams) honey or pure maple syrup

½ teaspoon pure vanilla extract

1. Position a rack in the center of the oven and preheat the oven to 350°F. Have ready a 9-inch tart pan with a removable bottom set on a baking sheet (a 9-inch springform pan works, too, as does a shallow 9-inch pie plate if you're not concerned with removing the pie or tart from the pan before serving).

2. In the bowl of a food processor, combine half the nuts, the graham crackers, and salt. Process until the nuts are finely chopped and the grahams have been ground to fine crumbs.

3. In a small heatproof bowl, combine the butter, honey, and vanilla extract. Melt together in the microwave on high power for 30 to 40 seconds.

4. Pour the melted butter mixture over the crumbs in the processor. Blend until the mixture is evenly moistened and resembles wet sand. Add the rest of the nuts and pulse until finely chopped with a smattering of nutty bits throughout, with the largest pieces no bigger than ⅛ of an inch. Scrape the crumbs into the tart or pie pan. Use your hands to press the crust evenly across the bottom

TIP: *Depending on the type of graham crackers, nuts, and liquid sweetener you use, the crust mixture may have a bit more moisture in it and require a couple minutes longer of baking time. If the crust emerges from the oven looking soft and a bit puffed, simply remove it, gently press it back into shape using the measuring cup you used to initially shape the crust, and return it to the oven to bake for 2 more minutes.*

and about 1½ inches up the sides of the pan. Use a flat-bottomed measuring cup to smooth out the crust and press it firmly into the pan.

5. Bake until golden, fragrant, crisp at the edges, and dry on the surface, 10 to 12 minutes. Cool completely on a wire rack before filling.

NUTTY CHOCOLATE GRAHAM CRUST

Add 2 tablespoons (½ ounce/12 grams) unsweetened natural cocoa powder to the crackers and nuts in the first step of the recipe. Add 1 additional tablespoon of butter and 1 more tablespoon of honey or maple syrup.

NUTTY GINGERSNAP CRUST

Add ¾ teaspoon ground cinnamon, ¼ teaspoon ground ginger, and ⅛ teaspoon freshly grated nutmeg or allspice to the food processor before grinding the crackers and nuts.

Honeyed Hot Chocolate

MAKES TWO 1¼-CUP SERVINGS

This hot chocolate is awesome—lightly sweetened with a great interplay going on between the ambrosial honey and the rich, dark chocolate. The most fantastic thing is that you can use low-fat milk, and with the addition of a little cornstarch, you get something so unbelievably silky, you'd swear what you were drinking had a pound of chocolate and a gallon of cream. Phenomenal!

2 cups (16 ounces/454 grams) low-fat (1% or 2%) milk

1 teaspoon cornstarch

2 ounces (57 grams) bittersweet chocolate (60% to 70% cacao), chopped

2 tablespoons (1½ ounces/42 grams) honey

Generous pinch of fine sea salt

1. Put ¼ cup of the milk into a small bowl. Whisk in the cornstarch until dissolved and set aside.

2. In a small saucepan, combine the remaining milk, chocolate, honey, and salt. Place the pan over medium heat. Whisk often until the chocolate has completely melted. Stir in the cornstarch mixture. Continue whisking occasionally until the hot chocolate looks as though it's just about to come to a boil—you'll see the surface of the liquid start to rumble from within just a bit. A moment later, the cornstarch should start to do its thing, and you'll notice the thickness of the hot chocolate suddenly change. Before the mixture comes to a full boil, remove the pan from the heat and cover to keep warm before serving.

TIP: *Try the hot chocolate with honeyed whipped cream. Pour ¼ cup (2⅛ ounces/60 grams) of heavy cream and 1 teaspoon of honey into a medium bowl. Use a handheld mixer to whip the cream to soft peaks. Pour the hot chocolate into 2 mugs and top with the honeyed whipped cream.*

HOW TO BLIND-BAKE A PIE CRUST

After the dough has been chilled, roll out the crust as directed and tuck it into a 9-inch pie plate or a 10-inch tart pan. Decoratively crimp the edges as you wish. Prick the bottom of the rolled and crimped crust all over with a fork. Freeze the crust in the pan for 10 to 15 minutes until firm. Position a rack in the lower third of the oven and preheat the oven to 350°F. Wrap the frozen crust completely in a large sheet of aluminum foil. Fill the plate with ceramic pie weights or dried beans. Bake for 15 minutes. Carefully remove the pie weights and aluminum foil from the crust. Return the crust to the oven and bake 15 minutes more, or until pale golden and dry to the touch. Cool completely before filling.

Whole Wheat All-Butter Pie Crust

MAKES 1 CRUST TO FIT A 9-INCH PIE PLATE OR A 10-INCH TART PAN

Whole wheat pie crust is a tricky thing. And by tricky I mean that it can have the tendency to taste and feel like that particleboard used to build college bookshelves. Thankfully, there's a way around the thudlike qualities of whole wheat pie crust without using white flour in the mix—the addition of cornstarch and a pinch of baking powder lightens this crust while still retaining the hearty nuttiness of whole wheat that complements so many naturally sweetened pie and tart fillings (and savory tarts and quiches, too!).

This crust is incredibly versatile, and I love to use it for recipes that require unbaked pastry, such as double-crust fruit pies, single-crust pies with a lovely lattice top, or even little portable hand pies. However, the two pie recipes in this book (see pages 98 and 108) both call for baking the crust before filling; you can find instructions for blind-baking this crust on the facing page.

1⅓ cups plus 1 tablespoon (6 ounces/168 grams) whole wheat pastry flour, spooned and leveled

1 tablespoon plus 1 teaspoon (⅜ ounce/11 grams) cornstarch

1 tablespoon evaporated cane juice

¼ teaspoon baking powder

¼ teaspoon fine sea salt

½ cup (1 stick/4 ounces/113 grams) unsalted butter, cold, cut into pieces

3 to 4 tablespoons (1½ to 2 ounces/43 to 57 grams) ice water

1. In the bowl of a food processor fitted with the steel blade, combine the flour, cornstarch, evaporated cane juice, baking powder, and salt. Pulse several times to blend. Toss in the chilled butter pieces and pulse to break the butter down into lima-bean-size bits—about 20 pulses. Add 3 tablespoons of the ice water and process briefly until the dough just begins to come together—if this takes more than 20 seconds or so, add 1 teaspoon of ice water at a time until the dough pulls off the sides of the processor bowl.

2. Line a work surface with plastic wrap. Turn out the dough onto the plastic. Gently shape it into a 5-inch disk. Wrap the dough tightly. Chill for at least 45 minutes. (The dough can be made and chilled up to 2 days before baking.)

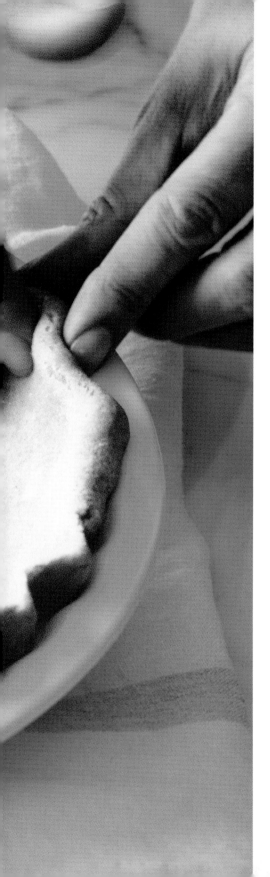

3. Lightly dust a work surface and rolling pin with no more than 1 tablespoon whole wheat pastry flour. (Unlike with all-purpose, too much whole wheat pastry flour when rolling out your pie dough can dry it out, so keep the dusting flour to a minimum.) Roll the dough to a ⅛-inch thickness and transfer to a 9-inch pie plate or 10-inch tart pan. Trim the edges and crimp a decorative edge. Fill and bake as directed by your recipe.

TIP: *This recipe makes a single crust. For a double-crust pie, simply double the amounts and divide the dough into 2 disks before wrapping and chilling.*

Acknowledgments

To my agent Judy Linden (and Team Stonesong), thank you for taking on a crazed mother of a newborn, believing in and helping to develop this concept, and always offering a kind ear and your wisdom.

Cassie Jones, I couldn't have asked for a more creative, whip-smart, and inspiring editor. Thank you for pushing this project forward, "getting it," and elevating my ideas from our very first conversation. To the entire team at William Morrow, thank you for your vision and enthusiasm for this book; I'm honored to be working with you.

To photographer Leigh Beisch and art director and stylist Sara Slavin—I am so happy that we got the dream team back together for number three! And to Tamara Rivera and James Ellerker, thank you for your awesome energy during a wild and crazy photo shoot. Special thanks to Sue Fisher King for loaning us additional, beautiful props.

Christine Gallary—thank you for your culinary genius, helping me with food styling, and saving the day on multiple occasions.

Rosie Alyea—my sister in juggling cookbook writing and mothering and ace recipe tester.

Sara Schilling—for cheering me on through every ambitious endeavor and offering your support, humor, and mad baking skills.

To countless friends who provided feedback and invaluable inspiration during the writing of this book, especially Darren McGraw, Matt Lewis, Luisa Weiss, Deb Perelman, Irvin Lin, and Elizabeth LaBau.

Big thanks to my incredible recipe-testing brigade of home bakers who enthusiastically sourced unusual ingredients and fired up their ovens from coast to coast: Megan Swearingen, Spring Utting, Hilary Ratner, Logan Levant, Katie Garber, Katie Rutledge, Whitney Berger, Margaret McGuire Novak, Jenny Panattoni, and Emily Larson.

A hearty thank-you to the readers of my blog, *Piece of Cake*, for your comments and positive vibes over the years.

To Stacey Greene, I couldn't have asked for a better second home for my baby boy so that I could work on this book. Thank you for being way more fun than me.

To my family, especially Mom and Tiff—thank you for always supporting me. To Gramma, who wrote down the original version of Mrs. Braun's Oatmeal Cookies for me years ago—your love, strength, and kindness will inspire me for the rest of my life.

To Scott, for taking on all those weekends of solo parenting and bolstering my confidence all the way through this book while we learned how to juggle two children together—I love you forever. And to Caroline and Andrew, thank you for making me crazy, bringing me such great joy, and happily eating all the cake.

Universal Conversion Chart

OVEN TEMPERATURE EQUIVALENTS

250°F = 120°C   400°F = 200°C

275°F = 135°C   425°F = 220°C

300°F = 150°C   450°F = 230°C

325°F = 160°C   475°F = 240°C

350°F = 180°C   500°F = 260°C

375°F = 190°C

MEASUREMENT EQUIVALENTS

Measurements should always be level unless directed otherwise.

⅛ teaspoon = 0.5 ml

¼ teaspoon = 1 ml

½ teaspoon = 2 ml

1 teaspoon = 5 ml

1 tablespoon = 3 teaspoons = ½ fluid ounce = 15 ml

2 tablespoons = ⅛ cup = 1 fluid ounce = 30 ml

4 tablespoons = ¼ cup = 2 fluid ounces = 60 ml

5⅓ tablespoons = ⅓ cup = 3 fluid ounces = 80 ml

8 tablespoons = ½ cup = 4 fluid ounces = 120 ml

10⅔ tablespoons = ⅔ cup = 5 fluid ounces = 160 ml

12 tablespoons = ¾ cup = 6 fluid ounces = 180 ml

16 tablespoons = 1 cup = 8 fluid ounces = 240 ml

Sources

WHOLESOME SWEETENERS

www.wholesomesweeteners.com

This company makes high-quality natural sweeteners, including nearly every sugar and liquid sweetener in this book. It also owns Billington's, which makes terrific muscovado. You can order through its website and take advantage of online coupons. There is even a Sugar Club, for which members can sign up and save on multiple purchases.

WHOLE FOODS

www.wholefoodsmarket.com

A treasure trove of natural ingredients, including a great bulk section. I'm especially fond of its 365 store brand, which has great turbinado and organic sugars and honey and maple syrup at good prices. Keep an eye out for online coupons to save on in-store purchases.

COSTCO

www.costco.com

This megastore has embraced natural sugars in recent years, and now carries high-quality pure maple syrup, multiple varieties of honey, agave nectar, organic cane sugar (evaporated cane juice), organic dairy, raw nuts and dried fruits, and even coconut sugar in bulk and at great prices.

CHEFMASTER

www.bkcompany.com

For my favorite natural food colorings; check the website for information on store locations and ordering.

INDIA TREE

www.indiatree.com

Purveyors of great specialty baking ingredients, including dark and light muscovado sugar, demerara sugar, and natural food colorings, along with a line of naturally colored sprinkles and decors.

MADHAVA

www.madhavasweeteners.com

Specializing in coconut sugar, agave nectars, and a wide variety of flavorful honeys, Madhava is especially well known for its coconut sugar, which is becoming widely available in mainstream supermarkets and can be found at Costco in bulk for a great price. Their monthly newsletter offers coupons and recipes.

RODELLE

www.rodellekitchen.com

A favorite source for insanely flavorful vanilla products, including beans, paste, and extracts, and high-quality spices and cocoa powders.

TRADER JOE'S

www.traderjoes.com

You have to be in certain parts of the United States in order to visit this wonderland, but you can't beat the prices on the majority of the natural foods at Trader Joe's, especially nuts, seeds, and dried fruits of all sorts. I also love its wide variety of colorful freeze-dried fruits.

LUNDBERG FAMILY FARMS

www.lundberg.com

Maker of my favorite brown rice syrup; it also offers online coupons.

KING ARTHUR FLOUR

www.kingarthurflour.com

Every baking ingredient you could possibly need, including great unbleached all-purpose flour, baking supplies, maple syrup, and maple sugar. It has a reliable online store as well as an active online community with invaluable baking advice and foolproof recipes.

COOMBS FAMILY FARMS

www.coombsfamilyfarms.com

A wonderful company that specializes in high-quality maple products, including a variety of maple syrups and maple sugar. I order its awesome maple sugar online through Amazon.

THE SWEET SORTER
Recipe Index by Sugar

If you're anything like me, you often find yourself with lots of little bags and boxes of baking ingredients purchased specifically for one recipe that somehow became buried and forgotten in the madness of a baker's pantry. Or perhaps one day, with a great sense of culinary adventure, you buy a giant container of an intriguing sugar and then get home and have no idea what the heck to do with it. This list calls out the recipes in this book by sugar, so if you ever happen to find yourself with a surplus of a certain sweetener, refer to the list below for inspiration to help you use it.

Maple Chocolate Cake 101

Maple Cloud Pudding 219

Maple Cream, Chocolate, and Walnut Tart 172

Maple Marshmallows 140

Maple Spun Sugar 157

Oat Jacks 56

Nutty Graham Crust 240

Soft, Fluffy Meringue 234

Spiced, Brûléed Maple Pumpkin Pie 108

MOLASSES

Bonfire Toffee Lollipops 160

Spiced Chocolate Molasses Buttons 83

ORGANIC CONFECTIONERS' SUGAR

Five-Flavors Party Cake 178

Iced Muscovado Caramel-Nut Blondies 73

My Favorite Vanilla Bean Buttercream 235

PILONCILLO, PANELA, JAGGERY

Crisp, Raw Sugar Meringue 231

Custard in Two Directions 217

Mango Lassi Frozen Yogurt 210

Piloncillo Dessert Waffles with Caramel Cream
    and Pan-Roasted Bananas 169

RAPADURA

Brigadeiros 149

Espresso, Rapadura, and Bittersweet Chocolate
    Semifreddo 211

Homemade Sweetened Condensed Milk 228

Mrs. Braun's Oatmeal Cookies 68

Oat Jacks 56

TURBINADO

Birdseed Brittle 154

Bonfire Toffee Lollipops 160

Brigadeiros 149

Buttermilk Caramel Sauce 225

Caramelized Praline Spread 151

Chocolate Chip Cookie Brittle 70

Chocolate, Cherry, and Cacao Nib Pavlova 182

Cinnamon-Sugared Blueberry Bundt 103

Crisp, Raw Sugar Meringue 231

Crunchy Almond Shortbread 80

Homemade Sweetened Condensed Milk 228

Mrs. Braun's Oatmeal Cookies 68

Next-Level Chocolate Chip Cookies 64

Nutty Honey Taffy 138

Oatmeal and Turbinado Cream Cookie
    Sandwiches 76

Orange-Scented Vanilla Bean and Turbinado
    Pound Cake 110

Piloncillo Dessert Waffles with Caramel Cream
    and Pan-Roasted Bananas 169

Pomegranate Candied Apples 131

Praline Cream Roulade 187

Raw Sugar and Mascarpone Caramels 144

Spiced Chocolate Molasses Buttons 83

Spiced, Brûléed Maple Pumpkin Pie 108

Strawberry and Lemon Cream Puffs 190

Index

NOTE: Page references in *italics* refer to photos.

C